ROYALWISE

QuickBooks Templates: Convenience Stores and Gas Stations

By Alicia Katz Pollock
Royalwise Solutions, Inc.
Intuit® Trainer/Writer Network
Elite QuickBooks® ProAdvisor®

Royalwise.com
503-406-6550

Published 2020 in the United States of America
ISBN 978-171714511-6

Dedication

I would like to dedicate this book to all of the independent convenience store and gas station operators out there, creating a road to a better life by keeping us on the move with supplies at our fingertips.

You are the people who drive the world, one happy customer at a time.

Table of Contents

Foreword

In January of 2017, my wife and I purchased a convenience store and gas station located on the 101 Coastal Highway in Reedsport, Oregon. Though I had years of experience owning and operating small businesses, as well as some bookkeeping experience, the purchase of Recreation Station highlighted the complexities of bookkeeping in a diverse retail atmosphere.

Frankly, it is amazing how many different products are sold through a modern convenience store & gas station. We purchased the business from a retiring couple that had been in the grocery/gas business for more than twenty years. Though it was obvious they were seasoned operators, many technology and systems had become available that they were not utilizing.

I knew that I needed to connect with someone who could help me learn more about the new technologies that might benefit the day-to-day bookkeeping activities that were happening on-site. After looking on the internet for a QuickBooks Professional, I came across some great reviews of Royalwise Solutions and Alicia Pollock. Alicia agreed to come to Reedsport from Portland and spend a couple days helping us...this turned into four.

We went through everything. Alicia listened to my current methods for each and every system (the processes left in place by the older retirees), and she helped come up with new tools, mostly utilizing QuickBooks Online.

She created Sales Receipts templates, Clearing Accounts, Charge Accounts, Recurring Transactions, Recurring Journal Entries, etc... Those made it easy to keep up with the books.

Another key implementation was creating limited login accounts for on-site managers, so that they could assist by entering daily sales and expense transactions. Even though they had access to enter this information, they did not have access to see our more private information such as bank balances, credit card balances, and reports.

Now, for the first time since we purchased the business, the managers were essentially keeping up with the books on a daily basis, vs. before, when as an owner, I would have to enter days (and sometimes weeks) worth of sales and expense data to get caught up to date. What a great feeling!

A second major implementation was her recommendation of a new electronic time clock program that would eliminate the hand-filled out timecards (yes, it was that antiquated). Our new T-Sheets iPad timeclock kiosk syncs with QuickBooks Online allowing us to easily do our own payroll each month.

Alicia Pollock has helped bring my vision for a smooth (bookkeeping) operating retail environment to reality. Any monies I have spent for her services were well worth it to the business, as well as for me personally, because she emphasized the learning aspect of her work, to teach me what I needed to know.

While Alicia still suggests that every business has a regularly scheduled bookkeeper to come in to make sense of the day, week, month, quarter, or year...for me, I needed to understand it, be able to do it, and manage it on my own. She taught me how to do the work and keep it up myself, which was exactly what I personally wanted. I'm glad I can turn to Alicia for assistance, for improvement of the system as it evolves, and to double-check my work a couple of times per year (most importantly after year's end).

This QuickBooks Template for Convenience Stores and Gas Stations is an actual copy of the structure of my store's books that we created, just with some of the categories renamed to make them more generic. You will reap the benefits of those four days we spent together, and get your own file started in just a few hours.

If you need additional help and training to implement the system, Alicia is great to work with and a pleasure to be around. You will not regret connecting with this professional to grow your business through bookkeeping and technology.

Thanks, Alicia, for putting this QuickBooks retail system together, and helping my business get off to a great start!!!!

Aaron Young
Owner, Recreation Station LLC

Acknowledgements

Special thanks to Aaron Young of Recreation Station in Oregon, who trusted me to overhaul his entire bookkeeping structure so he could analyze and grow his business. Thanks also to Zaira Papageorgiou of Bizambou, who refined my template for use with a Mobil station in Florida.

I'd like to thank Alison Ball and Donna Ohman from the Intuit Trainer/Writer Network for giving me the opportunity to reach a wider audience for my QuickBooks training and become a true QuickBooks Online Rock Star.

And of course, a shout out to Alex at Imagetrance for book cover design.

About this Template System

This QuickBooks template is based on two real Gas Station and Convenience Stores, Recreation Station on Highway 101 in Reedsport, Oregon; and a Mobil station in Plantation, Florida.

The owner of Recreation Station had recently bought the company, and wanted a brand-new QuickBooks file structure that allowed him to monitor not just sales and inventory, but also to make sure he was receiving proper payouts from other convenience store activities including the onsite ATM, WEX gas card payments, the Oregon Lottery, sales of Oregon Department of Fish and Wildlife permit sales, and bottle recycling returns.

He also maintained Charge Accounts for his employees who bought food and gas, as well as local businesses who only wanted to pay monthly.

This system includes a Chart of Accounts, Items Lists, Memorized Transactions, and the Memorized Reports needed for day-to-day operations.

It is designed to coordinate with your existing Point-of-Sale (POS) System. At the end of the day, run your POS System's Daily Sales Report or Z-Tape so that you have the numbers you need for sales departments and payment methods.

You or your managers enter that information into QuickBooks as a daily Sales Receipt. QuickBooks then runs sales reports, tracks inventory values, monitors Charge Accounts, and ensures you are getting reimbursed fairly by the lottery, ATM, and permit agencies.

If you have any questions about the setup or use of this system, please contact Alicia at http://www.royalwise.com, 503-406-6550. She is available to assist with implementation.

If you're interested in learning more about how a real convenience store and gas station successfully uses this QuickBooks template to manage its daily and monthly bookkeeping, please call business owner Aaron Young of Recreation Station in Reedsport, OR at (541) 706-1198.

Alicia also has a video course explaining how to set up your Gas Station and Convenience Store in QuickBooks Online. Check it out at http://royl.ws/QuickBooks-training-videos.

Buy the Ready-Made File

This book contains the setup information you need to create a QuickBooks file for your Convenience Store and Gas Station business.

You must have QuickBooks and bookkeeping experience to follow these instructions, as this book is not a tutorial on how to use QuickBooks or how to do bookkeeping. While we explain how to set up your file, we don't step you through click-by-click.

Even after implementing the instructions on these pages, it will take several hours to set up your QuickBooks file. If you would rather just open up your QuickBooks and be ready to go, a pre-made QuickBooks Desktop file is available for purchase from http://royl.ws/convenience-store-gas-station-template.

To use it, you will need a copy of QuickBooks Desktop 2019 or later.

If you would like to use the template with QuickBooks Online (QBO), you will need a subscription to QuickBooks Online Essentials or Plus. In order to upload the ready-made file into QuickBooks Online, you will also need a copy of QuickBooks Desktop for this one-time conversion. We suggest finding a trial copy, or asking a colleague who has QuickBooks Desktop to help you. Alicia can also provide this service! Book an appointment with her at http://royl.ws/schedule-with-Alicia.

Note that if you import the ready-made file into QuickBooks Online, you will need to recreate the Custom Reports by hand, as they do not import.

If you would like to purchase our ready-made QuickBooks Desktop file
to save you from having to set one up from scratch,
visit http://royl.ws/convenience-store-gas-station-template.

QBDT and QBO Terminology

This book has been written in terms of QuickBooks Premier or Pro for Desktop (QBDT), but there is no reason not to use the QuickBooks Online (QBO) version. In fact, we prefer it!

While most of the screen shots in this book come directly from our QuickBooks Template, the ones that demonstrate real data were taken from real Gas Station C-stores using QuickBooks Online. Hopefully, comparing the QBO screenshots to the Template's format won't be too confusing!

Here is a list of QuickBooks features mentioned in this book, and their corresponding terminology in both versions:

Desktop (Premier, Pro, Enterprise):	Online (Essentials or Plus):
Items	Products and Services
Memorized Transactions	Recurring Transactions
Memorized Reports	Custom Reports
Bill: Expenses tab (left)	Bill: Categories grid (top)
Bill: Items tab (right)	Bill: Items grid (bottom)

Case Study: Recreation Station

The Original QuickBooks Clean Up

I recently did a 50-hour project setting up QBO for a convenience store and gas station in Reedsport, OR. The owner, Aaron Young, had bought the business on the side of Hwy 101 on the Oregon Coast, and needed to set up his books. We took the previous owner's existing QB Desktop file and imported it into QBO. We cleaned up his structure and his numbers, reorganized the Chart of Accounts to reflect what he wanted to track, and customized Sales Receipts for steps he wanted his managers to perform.

Sales Receipts for Daily Sales

I created Sales Receipts for Z-Tapes at the end of the day instead of Journal Entries so that his shift managers could fill them in with their Customer and Sales-restricted User Accounts. To do this I created Products and Services that pointed to the income and expense areas of the Chart of Accounts. I customized a Recurring Daily Sale Receipt so that it was user-friendly for the managers, with instructions and explanations in the Descriptions.

A bonus to taking this approach is that Aaron could now run Product Sales Summary reports, and analyze how well each of his departments was doing.

Fuel Cost of Sales

His fuel costs were interesting. I discovered that the previous owner had been posting the state fuel tax into Inventory-Gas instead of COGS-Gas. After I reclassified them, the Inventory-Gas account periodically ran negative through the month, which wasn't right because they never ran out of gas in the tanks. To solve this, I had him find out as of 12/31 what the actual gallons were in the tanks on that day, and we researched the average price of December's deliveries. That told us how much Fuel Inventory he actually had.

To correct it, I transferred the difference from COGS back into Inventory. Now his Inventory-Gas account was exact. His COGS-Gas account was more accurate than the last owner's records. This reclassification caused his income and profit to go up $100,000!

ATM

Recreation Station has an ATM in the store. Aaron wanted to make sure the money declared by the bank actually matched the amount the machine gave out. Money from the cash drawer was transferred into the ATM, dispensed, and then reimbursed by the bank. I made an ATM Clearing Account to track the money in and out of the machine. By reconciling the account to zero every week, he could verify that he was being repaid accurately.

WEX Payments

I made a similar Clearing Account for his WEX payments. WEX is a gas card that corporate fleet drivers use as payment, and then WEX reimburses the money a few days later. This Clearing Account reassured Aaron that he was getting reimbursed for his sales. We made a Product & Service in QBO to serve as a Payment Method in the Daily Sales Z-Tape, which puts money in the Clearing Account, and when the money hits the bank it's transferred out of the Clearing Account. But WEX is a little difficult to reconcile. Sometimes the daily WEX payment matched the sales receipts, but on weekends, the company batched the three payments together.

Because reconciling WEX was a little more complex, we made an instructional video about how to manage WEX in QuickBooks Online (visit http://royl.ws/WEX). The steps shown in the video would also work for any payment method Clearing Account.

Oregon Lottery

We also created a similar Clearing Account for the OR Lottery, using a weekly Journal Entry to distribute the income, payouts, and state contributions.

Owner's Comp Gift Certificates

I set up an Owner's Comp system. For example, an employee accidentally broke the glass in a motorist's mirror. Aaron comped the driver $75 by giving him a redeemable gift certificate. I created a JE that moved the money from

Discount/Refunds Given to a Gift Certificate Liability. Every time the driver's Gift Certificate was redeemed, the Daily Sales Receipt reduced his $75 in the Liability account until it was gone.

Cash Drawer

The owner paid some small bills out of the till. Local hummus, firewood, night crawlers, and linen laundry were all paid in cash. The previous owner's system only reported that some cash was spent, but not for what. The new system pushed each product category to the proper COGS or Expense account.

Recurring Transactions Templates

As I created each data entry step, I saved the procedure's form as a Recurring Transaction. I named them Daily:, Weekly:, and Monthly:, with the reason for the transaction as the name. This way he could see what tasks needed to be done with what frequency.

As an added bonus, I also duplicated each one and appended "Backup" to the name. Because many of the transactions require small alterations when used, QuickBooks always asks if you want to save those changes to the Recurring Transaction template. If they accidentally clicked "Yes," they would lose the system we set up. As a safeguard, if that mistake was made, they could replace the bad template with the backup.

Delegate!

By crafting the gas station and convenience store's transaction structure so that as many transactions as possible could be done by managers with limited User Accounts (by making them Sales Receipts instead of Journal entries), Aaron could delegate many of his daily tasks, saving him time every day.

Setting Up QuickBooks

Chart of Accounts

The first step in getting up and running is to create your Chart of Accounts (COA). When you open up QuickBooks, it comes with a standard COA for you to modify.

Some of the categories are already be there waiting for you—these can be renamed to your liking. Some categories need to be added. Some you won't need, and they can be deleted.

Start by renaming existing accounts or adding new ones to match the screenshots below. Then delete any accounts that you're not using.

Sales Income, Inventory Assets, Cost of Goods, and your Items list are set up with a parallel structure. Every department in your C-store has income, inventory, cost of goods, and a product that's sold. This means that you'll see the same names repeatedly, but they all work together.

Use subcategory names that mirror the departments you have set up in your Point-of-Sale System.

Bank Accounts

Use the account type "Bank" for Checking, Savings, Tills, ATM, and Safe. Change the 4-digit number placeholders to the last 4 digits of your bank accounts to identify them easily.

NAME	TYPE
Cash on Hand	Bank
Cash in ATM	Bank
Cash in Tills	Bank
Safe Change Account	Bank
Checking - 1234	Bank
Clearing Accounts	Bank
ATM Clearing	Bank
Lottery Clearing	Bank
Wex Clearing	Bank
Savings - 5678	Bank

Create Clearing Accounts for ATM, Lottery, and WEX Payments. A "Clearing Account" is used to track money that goes in and out, equaling $0. It's used for money you outlay that will be later reimbursed by an outside agency. For example, your ATM dispenses $20, and the Vendor reimburses that $20. Clearing Accounts ensure you're getting back your outlay in full, minus any fees withheld.

Inventory

While technically you won't use QuickBooks' Inventory tools, all your purchases are Inventory Assets on your Balance Sheet as long as they're on your shelves waiting to be sold. Because Inventory is tracked by your POS system, there's no need to create a redundant log in QuickBooks. Instead of turning on the Inventory feature, simply record purchases to Inventory Assets, and manually make periodic Journal Entries (JE) to move your costs to Cost of Goods Sold (COGS) on your Profit & Loss Statement as merchandise sells.

Add your Inventory department categories as the type "Other Current Asset." This means the value there ebbs and flows frequently.

Inventory	Other Current Asset
Inventory-Alcohol	Other Current Asset
Inventory-Deli	Other Current Asset
Inventory-DFW	Other Current Asset
Inventory-Fuel	Other Current Asset
Inventory-Grocery	Other Current Asset
Inventory-Growlers	Other Current Asset
Inventory-Lottery	Other Current Asset
Inventory-Non Food	Other Current Asset
Inventory-Sporting Goods	Other Current Asset
Inventory-Store Supplies	Other Current Asset
Inventory-Tobacco	Other Current Asset

> **Be sure to buy ITEMS (QB) or PRODUCTS & SERVICES (QB Online) when you make bills, checks, and credit card charges for your purchases. Do NOT code the expenses directly to the Inventory or COGS account categories. Using the Items will put the value into Inventory.**

Every month, use the Memorized Journal Entry to transfer the cost of sales to the COGS categories, based on your margin percentage (see page 58). This is just an estimate based on your margin, and is accurate enough as long as your retail prices match the percentages.

Periodically (at least annually, if not quarterly or monthly), also do a hand count of your inventory, and make an Inventory Adjustment to true up your actual Inventory Current Asset of products in stock. Base this adjustment on your cost, NOT your sales price. This adjusts any margin discrepancies, as well as account for shrinkage.

Income Categories

Discounts/Refunds Given	Income
Fee Income	Income
Air Machine Income	Income
ATM Fee Income	Income
Bottle Return Fee Income	Income
DFW Fee Income	Income
Electric Vehicle Station	Income
Lottery Fee Income	Income
Incentives	Income
Grocery Incentives	Income
Tobacco Incentives	Income
Markup	Income
Miscellaneous Income	Income
Sales Income	Income
Sales-Alcohol	Income
Sales-ATV Permits	Income
Sales-Bottles Returns	Income
Sales-Deli	Income
Sales-DFW	Income
Sales-Fuel	Income
Sales-Grocery	Income
Sales-Growlers	Income
Sales-Lottery	Income
Sales-Non Food	Income
Sales-Sporting Goods	Income
Sales-Tobacco	Income
Sales of Product Income	Income
Unapplied Cash Payment Income	Income
Uncategorized Income	Income

Income is divided into categories for Fees, Incentives, and Sales Departments.

"Fee Income" is for all the money you are paid by the agencies who share with you a portion of their revenue.

"Incentives" are the money given to you by distributors for carrying or featuring certain products.

"Sales Income" are your C-store's departments, to track how much revenue you are making from your various product lines. Set these up to match your Point-of-Sale system.

You may choose to add additional detail. For example, you could break Alcohol into Beer & Wine, or separate your Grocery into detailed categories. Just be sure to create the necessary Income, Inventory Asset, and COGS categories for each one. See Appendix 3 on page 69.

Cost of Goods Sold

Merchandise

Cost of Goods Sold (COGS) is the actual cost of the merchandise that has gone out the door, based on the price you paid to acquire it.

Cost of Goods Sold	Cost of Goods Sold
Cash Drawer Payment to classify	Cost of Goods Sold
COGS-Alcohol	Cost of Goods Sold
COGS-ATV Permits	Cost of Goods Sold
COGS-Bottle Refunds	Cost of Goods Sold
COGS-Deli	Cost of Goods Sold
COGS-DFW	Cost of Goods Sold
COGS-Fuel	Cost of Goods Sold
COGS-Grocery	Cost of Goods Sold
COGS-Growlers	Cost of Goods Sold
COGS-Lottery	Cost of Goods Sold
COGS-Non Food	Cost of Goods Sold
COGS-Sporting Goods	Cost of Goods Sold
COGS-Tobacco	Cost of Goods Sold

As described in Inventory above, use the Monthly Memorized Transaction to transfer Inventory Assets to COGS (see page 58).

Some purchases, like permits and Carwash, don't have any inventory, so you can code those expenses straight to COGs.

Fuel

Set up a separate section for costs associated with Fuel delivery:

NAME	TYPE
Fuel Costs	Cost of Goods Sold
Fuel Delivery Charges	Cost of Goods Sold
Fuel Taxes	Cost of Goods Sold
Fuel Utility Costs	Cost of Goods Sold

Expenses

Standard business overhead expenses. You are welcome to rename the categories as you see fit.

Advertising and Promotion	Expense
Automobile Expense	Expense
Bank Charges	Expense
Bank Service Fees	Expense
Merchant Service Fees	Expense
Wex Fees	Expense
Business Licenses and Permits	Expense
Cash Over and Short	Expense
Charitable Contributions	Expense
Computer & Technology	Expense
Depreciation Expense	Expense
Dues & subscriptions	Expense
Guaranteed Payments	Expense
Guaranteed Payments Member #1	Expense
Guaranteed Payments Member #2	Expense
Interest Expense	Expense
Liability Insurance	Expense
Life Insurance Exp	Expense
Meals and Entertainment	Expense
Miscellaneous Expense	Expense
Office Supplies	Expense
Other Miscellaneous Service Cos	Expense
Payroll Expenses	Expense
Payroll Fees	Expense
Payroll Taxes	Expense
Wages	Expense
Postage	Expense
Professional Fees	Expense
Rent Expense	Expense
Repairs and Maintenance	Expense
Store Supplies	Expense
Taxes and Licenses	Expense
Travel	Expense
Unapplied Cash Bill Payment Exp	Expense
Uncategorized Expense	Expense
Utilities	Expense
Workers Compensation Ins.	Expense

Items List

Items are all used in the Memorized Transactions that are run daily, monthly, and annually. Even though they look very much like the categories in the Chart of Accounts, they are necessary so that you can use QuickBooks's forms in your daily workflow to buy and sell actual products.

When you create these items, point their Income accounts to the Income categories on the Chart of Accounts. Point their Expense to the proper Inventory Asset or Cost of Goods account.

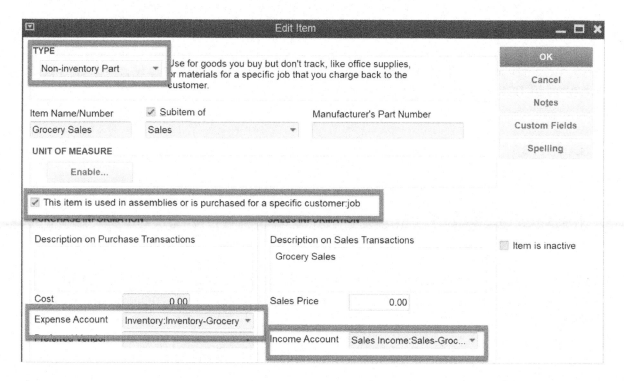

Sales

Sales by Department, used on the Daily Sales Z-Tape and on purchase expenses. Name your categories to match your Point-of-Sale System.

Point each Item's Income Account to the appropriate Sales Income department.

For purchases of tangible goods, point the COGS Account category to the corresponding Inventory Asset account.

If the products are not physical items, like permits and carwash supplies, point them directly to Cost of Goods.

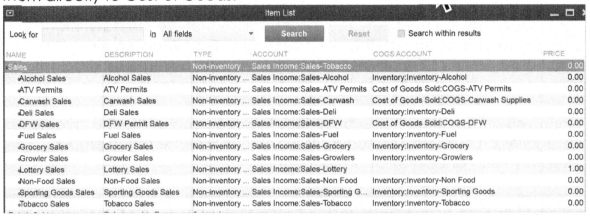

You may choose to include subcategories for more detailed reporting. See Appendix 3 on page 69 for an example.

Incentives

Incentives are Service Items used for income and sales from bottle returns, Fish & Wildlife permits, Electric Vehicle Stations (EVS), and retail incentives like Tobacco.

Incentives only use Sales categories, and don't have any associated purchase accounts.

Payment Methods

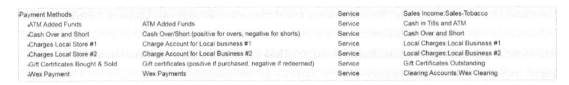

Payment Methods are Service Items used as subtractions on the Daily Sales Z-Tape to show how you received payment.

Payment methods only utilize Sales categories, and don't have any associated purchase accounts.

You also need Payment Methods for money going into the Checking Account, and for payments by Credit Card. In our Template these are set up as Payment Methods pointing to Undeposited Funds.

NAME	DESCRIPTION	TYPE	ACCOUNT
Checking Deposit		Payment	Undeposited Funds
Credit Card Total		Payment	Undeposited Funds

If you are using QuickBooks Online, include these as Service sub-items as shown on the list above.

If your Merchant Services is managed by your Fuel Vendor (see page 23), point Credit Card payments to a Clearing Account instead.

Payouts

Payouts		Service	Sales Income:Sales-Tobacco
ATM Dispensed	ATM Dispensed	Service	Cash in Tills and ATM
Bottle Return Payouts	Bottle Returns	Service	Cost of Goods Sold:COGS-Bottle Refunds
Charitable Donation Payout	Fundraiser, raffle, donations from Cash Drawer	Service	Charitable Contributions
Growler Payouts	Keg returns	Service	Inventory:Inventory-Growlers
Lottery Payouts	Lottery Payouts	Service	Cash in Tills and ATM
Misc Cash Drawer Payout	Enter description here	Service	Cost of Goods Sold:Cash Drawer Payment to clas...
Store Supplies Payouts	Local store supply purchases from Cash Drawer	Service	Store Supplies

Payouts refer to money taken out of the cash register and given to customers for Bottle Returns, Charitable Contributions, and Lottery winnings. It also includes cash paid to local Vendors, like the guy who washes your windows (Repairs and Maintenance).

This section also includes a category for money added to the ATM.

Payouts Service Items subtract money that would have been in the Cash Drawer. They only use Sales categories, and don't have any associated purchase accounts.

Daily Workflow

Convenience Store (C-Store)

Because your Point-of-Sale system tracks sales by department, there is no need to replicate the same detail in your QuickBooks. It's sufficient to run your POS Daily Sales Report (frequently called a Z-Tape), and copy it into QuickBooks.

Please see Appendix 2 on page 66 for a full copy of a POS Z-Tape Report.

A Z-Tape breaks out all your sales by department, then distributes the income by all the ways you took payment. This moves the money where it belongs in your QuickBooks, whether it's a checking account, a Clearing Account, or your cash drawer.

By creating a Memorized Transaction called "Daily Sales Receipt," you can easily replicate this breakdown in your QuickBooks.

Some people use a Journal Entry instead of a Sales Receipt. I prefer a Sales Receipt because then an employee with a limited User Account can still enter the transaction. Only the Master Administrator (typically the business owner) can make a Journal Entry.

In order to use a Sales Receipt, you have to take the extra step of creating Items for all the sales departments and payment methods (see page 11). The additional benefit is that now you can run profitability reports for each of your departments, because you're using the same Item for tracking income and purchases.

Setup

The top shows all the departments you have set up in your POS system. Enter the sales totals as positive numbers.

Edit the line items to change names to your own. Delete any you don't use.

Below that, enter all your Payment methods as negative numbers. These include credit cards and WEX payments. Cash and Checks become "Checking Account Deposit," and should match your actual deposit into the bank that day.

There are additional placeholders for:

- Each employee's charges for their store purchases that get deducted from payroll.
- Local business House Accounts.
- Purchases paid directly from the cash drawer. These include local Vendors who provide you with food and goods (for example, homemade food, night crawlers).
- Charitable Contributions from the cash drawer.
- Repairs and Maintenance paid from the cash drawer.
- Lottery payouts and bottle returns.
- Store supplies and other inventory if you run to another store to buy products you're out of.
- Money added to the ATM.
- Gift Certificates bought and redeemed.
- Cash Over and Short.

Workflow

Daily Sales Receipt

Run this Z-Tape transaction every day to match your Point-of-Sale System. It always equals $0, because the money you make each day is distributed out to the payment methods used to make the purchases.

I think of it as "Here's the money I got, where did it go?"

At the top are all the Sales, broken down by Departments.

Below that, the forms of payment are subtracted: how much was paid by credit card, cash, charged on account, and taken out of the cash drawer.

If you don't pay Vendors and suppliers out of your cash drawer, or have Charge Accounts for your employees, this Sales Receipt will be much shorter!

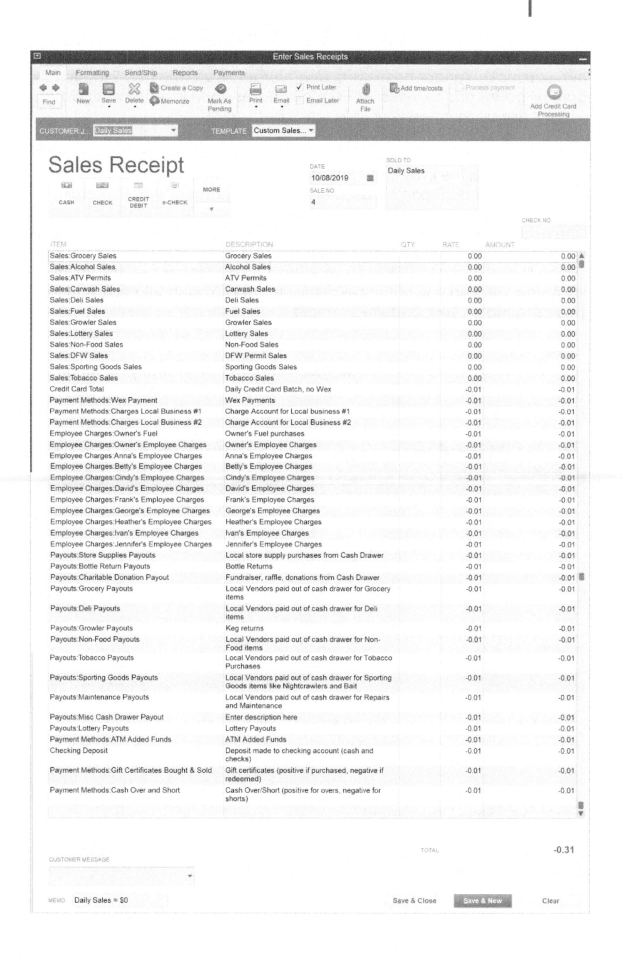

Sales Receipt

DATE 10/08/2019
SALE NO 4
SOLD TO Daily Sales

CASH CHECK CREDIT DEBIT e-CHECK MORE

CHECK NO

ITEM	DESCRIPTION	QTY	RATE	AMOUNT
Sales:Grocery Sales	Grocery Sales		0.00	0.00
Sales:Alcohol Sales	Alcohol Sales		0.00	0.00
Sales:ATV Permits	ATV Permits		0.00	0.00
Sales:Carwash Sales	Carwash Sales		0.00	0.00
Sales:Deli Sales	Deli Sales		0.00	0.00
Sales:Fuel Sales	Fuel Sales		0.00	0.00
Sales:Growler Sales	Growler Sales		0.00	0.00
Sales:Lottery Sales	Lottery Sales		0.00	0.00
Sales:Non-Food Sales	Non-Food Sales		0.00	0.00
Sales:DFW Sales	DFW Permit Sales		0.00	0.00
Sales:Sporting Goods Sales	Sporting Goods Sales		0.00	0.00
Sales:Tobacco Sales	Tobacco Sales		0.00	0.00
Credit Card Total	Daily Credit Card Batch, no Wex		-0.01	-0.01
Payment Methods:Wex Payment	Wex Payments		-0.01	-0.01
Payment Methods:Charges Local Business #1	Charge Account for Local business #1		-0.01	-0.01
Payment Methods:Charges Local Business #2	Charge Account for Local Business #2		-0.01	-0.01
Employee Charges:Owner's Fuel	Owner's Fuel purchases		-0.01	-0.01
Employee Charges:Owner's Employee Charges	Owner's Employee Charges		-0.01	-0.01
Employee Charges:Anna's Employee Charges	Anna's Employee Charges		-0.01	-0.01
Employee Charges:Betty's Employee Charges	Betty's Employee Charges		-0.01	-0.01
Employee Charges:Cindy's Employee Charges	Cindy's Employee Charges		-0.01	-0.01
Employee Charges:David's Employee Charges	David's Employee Charges		-0.01	-0.01
Employee Charges:Frank's Employee Charges	Frank's Employee Charges		-0.01	-0.01
Employee Charges:George's Employee Charges	George's Employee Charges		-0.01	-0.01
Employee Charges:Heather's Employee Charges	Heather's Employee Charges		-0.01	-0.01
Employee Charges:Ivan's Employee Charges	Ivan's Employee Charges		-0.01	-0.01
Employee Charges:Jennifer's Employee Charges	Jennifer's Employee Charges		-0.01	-0.01
Payouts:Store Supplies Payouts	Local store supply purchases from Cash Drawer		-0.01	-0.01
Payouts:Bottle Return Payouts	Bottle Returns		-0.01	-0.01
Payouts:Charitable Donation Payout	Fundraiser, raffle, donations from Cash Drawer		-0.01	-0.01
Payouts:Grocery Payouts	Local Vendors paid out of cash drawer for Grocery items		-0.01	-0.01
Payouts:Deli Payouts	Local Vendors paid out of cash drawer for Deli items		-0.01	-0.01
Payouts:Growler Payouts	Keg returns		-0.01	-0.01
Payouts:Non-Food Payouts	Local Vendors paid out of cash drawer for Non-Food items		-0.01	-0.01
Payouts:Tobacco Payouts	Local Vendors paid out of cash drawer for Tobacco Purchases		-0.01	-0.01
Payouts:Sporting Goods Payouts	Local Vendors paid out of cash drawer for Sporting Goods items like Nightcrawlers and Bait		-0.01	-0.01
Payouts:Maintenance Payouts	Local Vendors paid out of cash drawer for Repairs and Maintenance		-0.01	-0.01
Payouts:Misc Cash Drawer Payout	Enter description here		-0.01	-0.01
Payouts:Lottery Payouts	Lottery Payouts		-0.01	-0.01
Payment Methods:ATM Added Funds	ATM Added Funds		-0.01	-0.01
Checking Deposit	Deposit made to checking account (cash and checks)		-0.01	-0.01
Payment Methods:Gift Certificates Bought & Sold	Gift certificates (positive if purchased, negative if redeemed)		-0.01	-0.01
Payment Methods:Cash Over and Short	Cash Over/Short (positive for overs, negative for shorts)		-0.01	-0.01

TOTAL -0.31

CUSTOMER MESSAGE

MEMO Daily Sales = $0

Save & Close   Save & New   Clear

Monthly: Inventory to COGS Adjustment

When you make Vendor purchases, don't forget to use the ITEMS tab to record all goods and services. All Item purchases go to Inventory, an Other Current Asset account on your Balance Sheet.

Because this template is designed to work with a Point-of-Sale System, you're not actually using the Inventory features of QuickBooks. Instead, calculate the $ to transfer each month based on each department's profit margin.

At the end of each month, use the Monthly Memorized Transaction to create a Journal Entry that moves the cost of items sold out of Inventory on your Balance Sheet, and into COGS on your Profit & Loss Statement. The Journal Entry memos remind you of the percentages used. You should adjust these amounts to match your preferred margin.

C-Store

The .75 on the first line of the image below means that 75% of your monthly sales income was your cost to buy the product, and the remaining 25% is your profit margin.

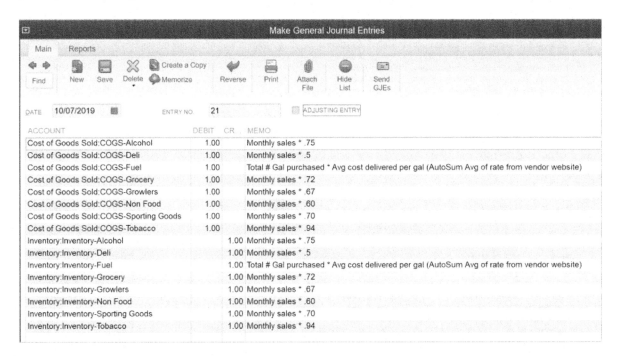

To use this Journal Entry, run a Profit & Loss Statement for your total sales for the month by Sales Department.

Each Debit/Credit field is a mini calculator! Enter the total sales, asterisk, margin, tab. The end result will be your cost.

Credit that total to your Inventory Asset and Debit your COGS.

You can, of course, do an actual physical inventory to move actual costs if you prefer.

Fuel
If your Fuel reports provide your actual COGS, enter that exact number.

Otherwise, the Fuel % should be adjusted based on the average cost of fuel sold, based on the Vendor's reports.

Take a look at the Monthly Fuel Workflow on page 30.

Annually (or more often): Inventory Adjustment for Shrinkage

Because your Monthly Inventory Adjustment is based on margin estimates instead of actual inventory counts, it's important to periodically square up your numbers. Use this Adjusting Journal Entry to compensate for theft, loss, and expired products.

I have the Memorized Transaction titled "Annual," but I recommend you do this quarterly, or as often as you want your reports to be completely accurate!

Instead of moving Inventory Assets to COGS, it moves the Inventory Adjustment to Shrinkage COGS. That way you can monitor shrinkage separately from your routine purchases on your Profit & Loss Statement.

Because you are not tracking Inventory in QuickBooks, this process takes some calculating on your part. Your POS system should be able to report your actual Inventory Quantity counts.

The first step is to perform a formal Inventory count of the products on your shelves. In the Reports Center under Inventory, there's a Physical Inventory Worksheet to print out and use.

Once you know the exact quantity of product on your shelves, calculate how much that inventory cost you to purchase (NOT the retail value of the items!). Subtract that value from the Inventory Asset value listed on your Balance Sheet for each department.

Use the Memorized Transaction to transfer that difference to your Inventory Adjustment/Shrinkage COGS account.

When you're done, the total value in the Inventory Assets on your Balance Sheet should be accurate.

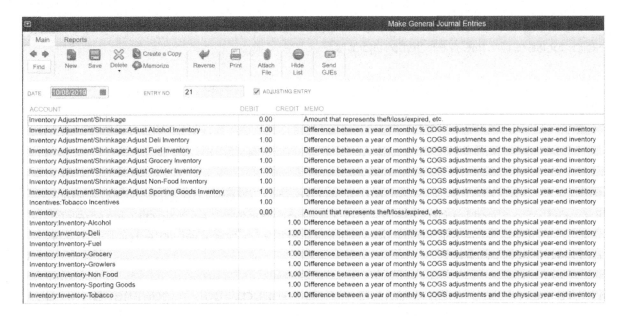

Fuel

Setup

Choose Inventory vs. Noninventory

Noninventory. In this system, fuel is not tracked as Inventory. While each purchase still goes to Inventory Assets, a monthly Journal Entry (described on page 18) moves the cost to Cost of Goods Sold. You can also run this Memorized Transaction any time you need to correct any quantity discrepancies.

Inventory. The benefit of using QuickBooks's Inventory tools to calculate Fuel Inventory Assets is that the Daily Sales Receipt automatically transfers sales cost into Cost of Goods Sold (using average cost in QB Desktop and FIFO in QBO).

Calculating Fuel sales using Inventory gets complex because you also need to make compensating adjustments if you carry Special grades. Because you mix together Unleaded and Super, then sell it as its own SKU, your fuel quantities are never correct.

If you choose to go this route, create Inventory Items for each fuel grade.

Cost of Goods Sold

See the Cost of Goods setup in the Chart of Accounts chapter on page 9. These fuel delivery and overhead expenses are separated from COGS-Fuel Sales for precise reporting.

If that's too much detail for your taste, you could code delivery charges and taxes directly to the COGS-Fuel Sales account instead.

Daily Workflow

In all these steps, be sure to use the Sales: Fuel Sales ITEMS to make sure the income and expenses fall into the correct categories on your Profit & Loss Statement and Balance Sheet.

Selling Fuel

On the Daily Sales Receipt (page 16), enter in the total gas sales for the day.

Our system combines them into one line for total Fuel sales, but if you would like to break out the day's sales into your station's grades, create additional Items and list them on multiple lines.

Purchasing Fuel

In the Expense where you enter your fuel purchases, be sure to click on the Items tab (Item Details grid in QBO) and use the Sales: Fuel Sales Item. This adds the cost to Inventory Asset and allows you to create Item profitability reports.

You may choose to enter one line for the total Gas purchase price, or enter multiple lines to track the quantity and cost of your various fuel grades: Unleaded, Super, and Diesel.

On the Expenses tab (Category Details grid in QBO), list your additional costs including delivery charges, taxes, and utility fees. Some gas companies may also charge you Mystery Shopper fees.

The image below is shown from QuickBooks Online to show which expenses are coded to Accounts directly, and which are entered as Items. In Desktop, the Accounts and Items tabs are side-by-side.

If your Merchant Services is through your Fuel Supplier
If you are a branded station, your gas supplier may also be your Vendor for Merchant Services. Every month they deduct your merchant service fees from your fuel charge, and you only pay the balance.

This complicates your workflow, because most months you buy more fuel than you take in credit card payments. But on some months, your credit card sales may be more than your fuel expense, and the supplier pays you!

Here is a sample monthly settlement that came out in the Gas Station's favor:

Date	Location	Reference No.	P.O No. or Additional Info	Original Amount	Discounts & Fees	Net Amount	Remaining Balance
06/25/2018	JACARANDA C/	INV-6247161806	DWS-1080883	5,604.81 6/25		5,604.81	
06/28/2018		EPLENTIF-36-R6282(	Credit Card Receipts	15,129.75	338.05-	14,791.70	
06/28/2018		EPLENTIF-3606-28-2	Credit Card Receipts	15,129.75-	338.05	14,791.70-	
06/28/2018		EPLENTIF-36628201:	Credit Card Receipts	15,129.75-	338.05	14,791.70-CCG 6/27	
06/29/2018		EPLENTIF-36629201:	Credit Card Receipts	15,726.71-	337.06	15,389.85-CC 6/28	
				Total Draft Amount:		24,576.54-	

New Transaction Summary	Subtotal	Amount	
Credit Cards		30,181.35-	
Gross Credit Cards	30,856.46-		
Credit Card Fees	675.11		
Fuel Sales		5,604.81	

Note that if you're using our Template, the Clearing Account is already set up in case you need it, but the Credit Card Payment method is still in the Daily Sales Memorized Transaction. Change it as described below.

What is happening is that every time you run your Daily Sales Receipt and specify how much of the day's sales was paid by credit card, that dollar amount goes into the Credit Card Payments Clearing Account, because you don't have the money yet.

This line on the Fuel Bill takes the money back out of the Clearing Account. The Clearing Account should zero out if the company is paying back accurately.

I like to reconcile the Clearing Account to $0 every month, but this can be challenging if the company takes a long time to reimburse you.

There are separate instructions for QuickBooks Desktop and QuickBooks Online:

In QuickBooks Desktop

Setup

In this scenario, Merchant Services also requires a Clearing Account because customers paid by credit card, and you need to confirm how much the company is supposed to reimburse YOU!

1. Add a new Bank account to the Chart of Accounts under the Clearing Accounts heading (see the instructions on page 6). In our template, we call it "Fuel Vendor CC Clearing" but I recommend using the Vendor name.

2. On the Items list (see image at right), instead of using a Payment Method for Credit Card Payments, create a Service Item and point both the Income and Purchase sections to this new Clearing Account.

3. Update your Daily Sales Receipt and replace the Credit Card Payments line with this one instead.

4. Create a new Item for Credit Card Merchant Service Fees as shown at right.

Workflow

There are two scenarios that come into play:
*   Your fuel purchases were more than your credit card sales, and you pay the supplier.
*   Your fuel purchases were less than your credit card sales, and the supplier pays you.

When you spend more on fuel purchases, and you pay the Fuel Supplier

This is fairly straightforward. Pay the expense using your checking account or credit card using a Bill. Be sure to use both tabs. This transaction is saved in Memorized Transactions as "Fuel Purchases":

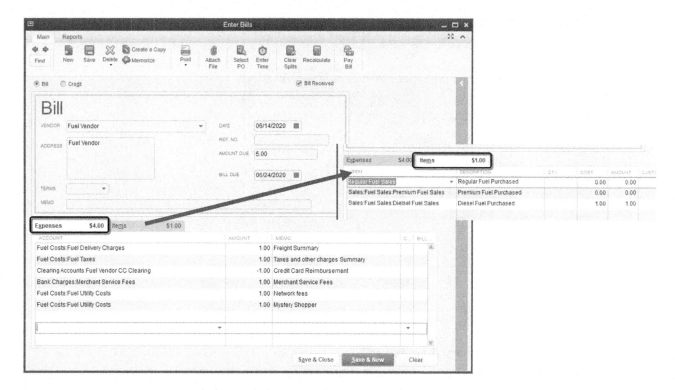

There's a line to specify the Merchant Service Fees.

The line that says, "Clearing Accounts: Fuel Vendor CC Clearing." That is how much the Fuel Company is paying you for your credit card sales. It's negative because they're deducting the amount from how much you have to pay them for your fuel delivery.

There is also a line for their Merchant Service Fees.

When your credit card sales are higher than your fuel purchases, and the Fuel Supplier pays you
You will use a Sales Receipt instead of an expense for your Fuel purchases, because the net is positive. Enter them with negative numbers, and the expenses will be recorded properly in Cost of Goods as usual.

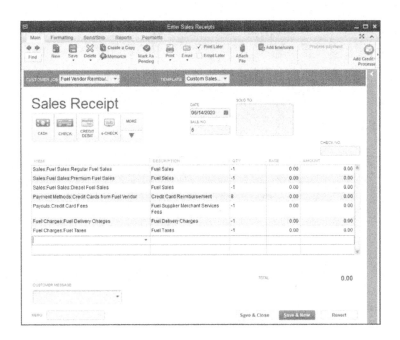

Add additional Deposit lines for:
- The total amount of credit card sales they are reimbursing you. Use the Credit Cards Clearing Account. This line will be positive.
- Subtract merchant service fees.
- Make adjustments for any additional line items, like Fuel Delivery, Taxes, and Incentives.

The grand total at the bottom shows that you received more in credit card sales than you bought in fuel.

In QuickBooks Online

Setup
In this scenario, Merchant Services also requires a Clearing Account because customers paid by credit card, and you need to confirm how much the company is supposed to reimburse YOU!

Add a new Bank account to the Chart of Accounts under the Clearing Accounts heading (see the instructions on page 6). In our template, we call it

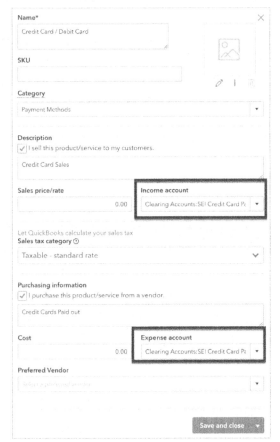

"Fuel Vendor CC Clearing" but I recommend using the Vendor name.

On the Items list (see image at right), instead of using a Payment Method for Credit Card Payments, create a Service Item and point both the Income and Purchase sections to this new Clearing Account instead of Undeposited Funds (this image is from QuickBooks Online, since our template is not designed for this workflow).

Workflow

There are two scenarios that come into play:

- Your fuel purchases were more than your credit card sales, and you pay the supplier.
- Your fuel purchases were less than your credit card sales, and the supplier pays you. This takes several steps to manage.

When you spend more on fuel purchases, and you pay the Fuel Supplier

This is fairly straightforward. Pay the expense using your checking account or credit card:

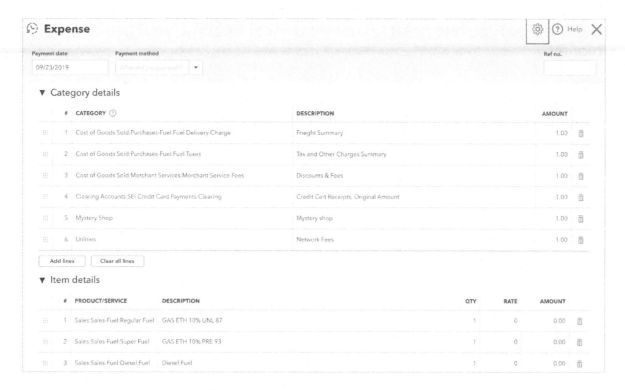

There's a line to specify the Merchant Service Fees.

Note the line that says, "Clearing Accounts: SEI Credit Card Payments Clearing."[1] That is how much the Fuel Company is paying you for your credit card sales. It's negative because they're deducting the amount from how much you have to pay them for your fuel delivery.

What is happening here is that every time you run your Daily Sales Receipt and specify how much of the day's sales was paid by credit card, that dollar amount goes into the Credit Card Payments Clearing Account, because you don't have the money yet.

This line on the Fuel Bill takes the money back out of the Clearing Account. The Clearing Account should zero out if the company is paying back accurately.

I like to reconcile the Clearing Account to $0 every month, but this can be challenging if the company takes a long time to reimburse you.

When your credit card sales are higher than your fuel purchases, and the Fuel Supplier pays you
This process takes two steps, because you still have to run your total Fuel Expenses, but you also need to make a deposit because you're receiving money.

Step 1:
Create a standard Fuel Purchase Expense as described on page 22. The difference is that you will "pay" it out of Undeposited Funds:

---

[1] In this case, SEI is the name of the supplier, but in our Template the Clearing Account was called "Fuel Vendor CC Payments. Feel free to customize yours!

Step 2:
Make a Bank Deposit to your Checking Account for the amount of credit card sales the company is reimbursing you for.

When you start the Bank Deposit, select the Expense created in Step 1 above.

Then manually add additional Deposit lines for:
- The total amount of credit card sales they are reimbursing you. Use the Credit Cards Clearing Account.
- Subtract merchant service fees.
- Make adjustments for any additional line items, like Fuel Incentives.

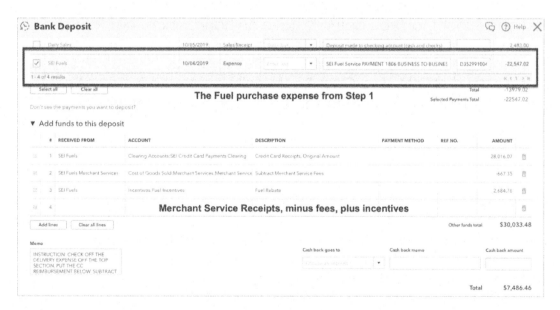

The grand total at the bottom shows that you received more in credit card sales than you bought in fuel.

Monthly Workflow

Every month you'll need to adjust your books to account for the cost of your fuel sold, compared to how much you have in your tanks.

Noninventory

Use the Monthly Adjustment Journal Entry described on page 18 to account for Fuel. To get the numbers for the transaction, multiply the total purchases (all suppliers' total cost for month) and divide by number of gallons of all products (diesel, gas, premium, etc.). This gives you the average monthly cost per gallon.

Then multiply the Total # Gal sold * Avg cost delivered per gal. Enter this number in the correct lines in the transaction.

Inventory

Instead of using the Monthly Journal Entry described on page 18 to transfer that COGS value, most of the work has already been done for you by the Daily Sales Receipt – each sale of inventoried grades moves the money form Inventory Asset to COGS automatically.

But this doesn't account for Special grades. Your reports will show more Unleaded and Super than you actually have on hand, since the two were mixed together to sell a non-inventory Special Grade.

Instead of the Journal Entry, use QuickBooks's "Inventory Activities > Adjust Quantity/Value on Hand" feature to square up your gallons on hand for each grade.

Annual Workflow

If your Fuel is non-inventoried, use the Yearly Memorized Transaction to correct the estimates to your actual physical inventory. That is when you'll account for evaporation, shrinkage and theft.

The Lottery

This Journal Entry is based on the Florida Lottery. Your state may be different. Create it in based on the weekly lottery report you receive from your State.

In this example I have separate tracking for Lotto and Scratch-its. If your state doesn't do Lotto, skip those fields or delete them from the template.

Setup

The Chart of Accounts
Create these categories in the Chart of Accounts. The colon indicates which heading to group them under.

Fee Income: Lottery Fee Income
Income account for commissions you receive from the state.

Sales Income:Sales-Lottery
Income account for your total lottery ticket sales.

Cost of Goods Sold:COGS-Lottery
COGS account for the cost of the tickets you sold.

The Items List
These two categories are used on the Daily Sales Receipt to track Lottery Sales Income, and Payouts from the register for winning tickets.

Create them in the Items list to point to the corresponding Chart of Accounts categories. The colon indicates which heading to group them under.

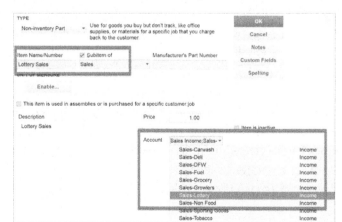

Sales: Lottery Sales
Your income from selling Lottery Tickets.

Payouts: Lottery Payouts

The cash you take out of the Till to pay customers for their Lottery Winnings.

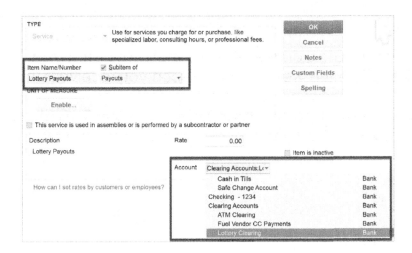

Point the account to your Lottery Clearing Account to ensure that the state reimburses you in full.

Workflow

Daily: Include the Lottery on the Daily Sales Receipt Z-Tape

When you create the Daily Sales Receipt, enter the Lottery income and Payouts.

Weekly: Lottery Journal Entry

Create and Memorize this General Journal Entry. Include the $1 placeholders in the Debit and Credit Columns so that you know where to enter the funds. Copy the Memos so that you remember what each line is for. Call it "Weekly: Lottery" so that you don't have to create it from scratch each week.

These line items in the Journal Entry (below) repeat because they mirror a typical Weekly Settlement Report you receive from the State (right). You don't need to create unique items for every line; instead, the sales and fees accumulate.

Be sure to write detailed Memos so that you understand what each line is for. Also include placeholder dollar amounts in the Debit and Credit columns, and suggestions in the memo, otherwise this weekly transaction gets extremely confusing.

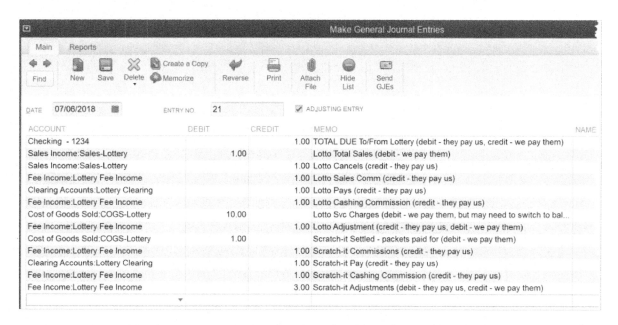

- **Checking** – Money paid to you by the State Lottery, and deposited into your Checking account. It may be a debit or credit depending if you gave out more in winnings than you took in.
- **Sales-Lottery** - total Lotto Sales, from your POS. There are two rows to account for any cancelled transactions.
- **Lottery Fee Income** - the commission Lotto pays you.
- **Lottery Clearing** – this zeros out the Clearing Account used to track how much you paid out for winning tickets, to ensure you are getting reimbursed.
- **COGS-Lottery** – Service Charges for Lotto. Typically, it's an expense you incur. Occasionally you get reimbursed and need to switch the column to Credit.
- **Lottery Fee Income** – sometimes the Lotto includes an "adjustment." This is a catch-all category in case you need it. It may be a debit or credit depending on the week.
- **COGS-Lottery** – Scratch-it packets you paid for
- **Lottery Fee Income** – Scratch-it Commissions
- **Lottery Clearing** - total Lottery Payouts you gave people from the cash register. Now you are getting reimbursed for those winning scratch-its. As before, this zeros out the Clearing Account.

- **Lottery Fee Income** – Scratch-it Commissions received
- **Lottery Fee Income** – An "adjustment" column in case you need it.
- **Utilities** – Some states charge line fees for connection (not shown).
- **COGS-Lottery** - reclaimed inventory, discounts, free tickets (not shown).

ATM

If you have an ATM on site, you refill it from your cash drawer as the money is dispensed. The ATM Vendor reimburses you for the funds. You also get a cut of the fees charged by the ATM Machine with each withdrawal.

Set up

The Chart of Accounts

Cash in ATM
There is a subcategory for ATM cash in the Cash on Hand header account.

ATM Clearing Account
Create an ATM Clearing Account as a Bank account so that you have an accurate verification that the ATM Vendor is reimbursing you properly. The money dispensed equals the money you are reimbursed by the ATM company, with an end result of a $0 net balance. For this reason, reconcile it to $0 every month.

NAME	TYPE
Cash on Hand	Bank
Cash in ATM	Bank
Cash in Tills	Bank
Safe Change Account	Bank
Checking - 1234	Bank
Clearing Accounts	Bank
ATM Clearing	Bank
Lottery Clearing	Bank
Wex Clearing	Bank
Savings - 5678	Bank

ATM Fee Income
Every month you receive a cut of the fees charged by the ATM when customers make withdrawals.

Create a Fee Income account in the Chart of Accounts.

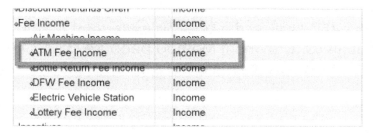

The Items List

Money Dispensed from the ATM

Every day, use the ATM's report to create a Sales Receipt for the money dispensed by the ATM that day. Create a Payouts Service Item that points to the Cash in ATM account.

This reduces the amount of cash onsite.

Wex Payment	Wex Payments	Service	Clearing Accounts:Wex Clearing	0.00
Payouts		Service	Sales Income:Sales-Tobacco	0.00
ATM Dispensed	ATM Dispensed	Service	Cash in Tills and ATM	0.00
Bottle Return Payouts	Bottle Returns	Service	Cost of Goods Sold:COGS-Bottle Returns	0.00
Charitable Donation Payout	Fundraiser, raffle, donations from Cash Drawer	Service	Charitable Contributions	0.00
Deli Payouts	Local Vendors paid out of cash drawer for Deli items	Service	Inventory:Inventory-Deli	0.00
Grocery Payouts	Local Vendors paid out of cash drawer for Grocery items	Service	Inventory:Inventory-Grocery	0.00
Growler Payouts	Keg returns	Service	Inventory:Inventory-Growlers	0.00
Lottery Payouts	Lottery Payouts	Service	Cash in Tills and ATM	0.00
Maintenance Payouts	Local Vendors paid out of cash drawer for Repairs and Maintenance	Service	Repairs and Maintenance	0.00
Misc Cash Drawer Payout	Enter description here	Service	Cost of Goods Sold:Cash Drawer Payment t...	-1....
Non-Food Payouts	Local Vendors paid out of cash drawer for Non-Food items	Service	Inventory:Inventory-Non Food	0.00
Sporting Goods Payouts	Local Vendors paid out of cash drawer for Sporting Goods items like Nightcrawl...	Service	Inventory:Inventory-Sporting Goods	0.00
Store Supplies Payouts	Local Vendors paid out of cash drawer for Store Supplies	Service	Store Supplies	0.00
Tobacco Payouts	Local Vendors paid out of cash drawer for Tobacco Purchases	Service	Inventory:Inventory-Tobacco	0.00

Money Used to Refill the ATM

Create an Item for ATM Added Funds as a Payment Method pointing at the Cash in Tills and ATM bank account. The Daily Sales Receipt contains a Payment Method for the ATM which takes the money out of the Till to put in the ATM machine.

Lottery		Service	Sales Income:Sales-Tobacco	
Payment Methods		Service	Sales Income:Sales-Tobacco	
ATM Added Funds	ATM Added Funds	Service	Cash in Tills and ATM	
Cash Over and Short	Cash Over/Short (positive for overs, negative for shorts)	Service	Cash Over and Short	
Charges Local Store #1	Charge Account for Local business #1	Service	Local Charges:Local Business #1	
Charges Local Store #2	Charge Account for Local Business #2	Service	Local Charges:Local Business #2	
Gift Certificates Bought & Sold	Gift certificates (positive if purchased, negative if redeemed)	Service	Gift Certificates Outstanding	
Wex Payment	Wex Payments	Service	Clearing Accounts:Wex Clearing	

Workflow

Daily: Include the ATM Refill on the Daily Sales Receipt Z-Tape

The ATM refill counts as a Payment Method because cash is taken out of the Till at the end of the day to move into the ATM machine.

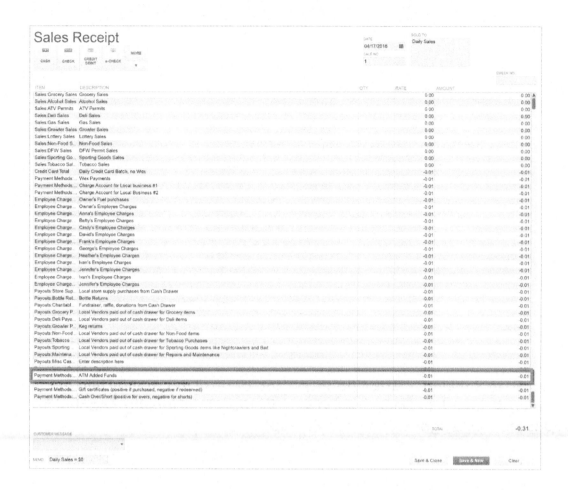

Daily: ATM Dispensed

Run a report daily from your ATM. Use this Sales Receipt to record how much money was dispensed that day.

Create a Sales Receipt. The Customer is "ATM." Use the "Payouts:ATM Dispensed" Item, and enter that day's total.

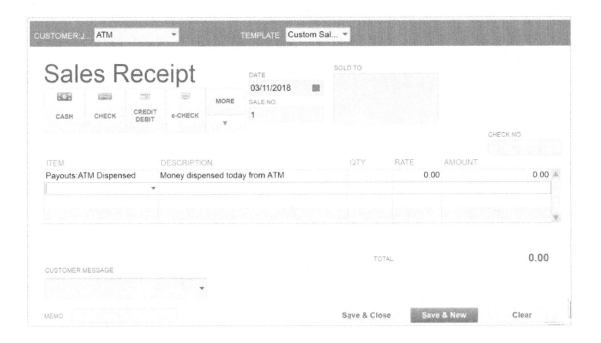

Important: Go to Banking > Make Deposits, and deposit this money into the ATM Clearing Account. In QBO, instead specify the ATM Clearing Account in the "Deposit to:" field right in the Sales Receipt.

Depositing into the Clearing Account offsets the money put into the ATM from your Daily Sales Receipt Z-Tape.

This tracks how much money left the store, and you use the Clearing Account to verify that the ATM company is reimbursing you properly.

Daily: Get reimbursed by the ATM company
When you receive reimbursements from the company a few weeks later, use a Transfer from the ATM Clearing Account to your Bank. This zeros out the ATM Clearing Account.

This is a great use for Banking Rules – automate this transaction so that when it shows up your Banking Feed, you don't need to create the Transfer manually. It just enters itself!

Monthly: Reconcile the ATM Clearing Account

Reconcile the ATM Clearing Account to $0 every month by checking off the matching money dispensed and reimbursed. Note that the dates will probably be several weeks apart.

Keep an eye out for any disbursements that never received an equal reimbursement. To date we have never seen any, but the ATM Clearing Account ensures that you'll notice any issues.

Monthly: Receive payments for your portion of the ATM Fees

When the ATM company pays you your portion of the ATM fees, make a Deposit using the "Fee Income:ATM Fee Income" account category.

This can be pulled in through the Banking Feed.

Car Wash

If you have a Carwash on site, count the Income as a Sales department in your POS. Supplies go straight to Cost of Goods Sold, not Inventory. Repairs and Maintenance has its own separate Expense account.

Set up

The Chart of Accounts

Carwash Income
Create a Carwash Sales Income account in the Chart of Accounts.

Carwash Cost of Goods Sold
Create a Carwash COGS in the Cost of Goods section of your Chart of Accounts. This is where you put all your supplies used up while providing Carwash services (soap, chemicals, supplies).

Sales Income	Income
Sales-Alcohol	Income
Sales-ATV Permits	Income
Sales-Bottles Returns	Income
Sales-Carwash	Income
Sales-Deli	Income
Sales-DFW	Income
Sales-Fuel	Income
Sales-Grocery	Income
Sales-Growlers	Income
Sales-Lottery	Income
Sales-Non Food	Income
Sales-Sporting Goods	Income
Sales-Tobacco	Income
Sales of Product Income	Income
Unapplied Cash Payment Income	Income
Uncategorized Income	Income
*Cost of Goods Sold	Cost of Goods Sold
Cost of Goods Sold	Cost of Goods Sold
Cash Drawer Payment to cla...	Cost of Goods Sold
COGS-Alcohol	Cost of Goods Sold
COGS-ATV Permits	Cost of Goods Sold
COGS-Bottle Refunds	Cost of Goods Sold
COGS-Carwash Supplies	Cost of Goods Sold
COGS-Deli	Cost of Goods Sold
COGS-DFW	Cost of Goods Sold
COGS-Fuel	Cost of Goods Sold
COGS-Grocery	Cost of Goods Sold
COGS-Growlers	Cost of Goods Sold

Carwash Maintenance and Repair
Create a Carwash Repair and Maintenance Expense account for all work done to maintain and operate the Carwash. You can put durable supplies and overhead expenses here as well.

Rent Expense	Expense
Repairs & Maintenance - Carwash	Expense
Repairs and Maintenance	Expense
Store Supplies	Expense

The Items List

Carwash Sales

Create a Carwash Sales Item to track both the Income and COGS expenses. Use the type Non-inventory Part even though it's more of a Service, just so it can be grouped with other Sales departments.

Make it a subcategory of Sales Income.

In the Purchase information, choose the COGS account for Carwash Supplies.

In the Income Account box, choose your Sales-Carwash Income category.

This way you can also use Items to buy your Carwash supplies, and run profitability reports on the Carwash!

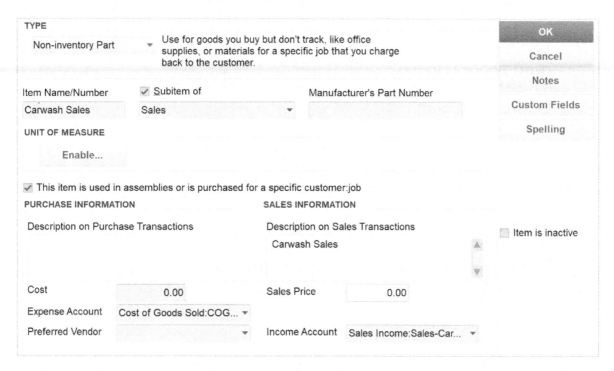

Workflow

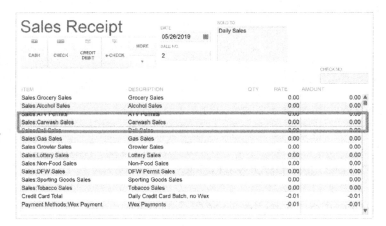

Daily: Include the Carwash Sales on the Daily Sales Receipt Z-Tape

This total comes from your Point-of-Sale System's Daily Report.

Daily: Classify Expenses

Any purchases related to the Carwash fall into two categories:

1. Supplies that get used up: Use the Carwash Sales in the Items tab in your Expense transaction. This already points to the Cost of Goods Sold Carwash account.

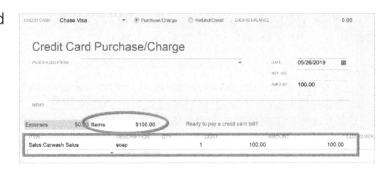

2. For any durable goods used for ongoing maintenance, use the Expenses tab and the Repairs & Maintenance – Carwash account.

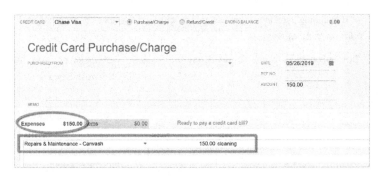

Employee & Owner Charges

Many convenience store employees buy snacks, gas, and cigarettes from you. You may choose to have them just pay outright at the time, but many stores track their purchases and deduct them from payroll.

Aaron jokes that he prefers Charge Accounts because it aids with employee retention. His team members don't want to quit because then they'll owe him money. In fact, Aaron says that if he notices a change in their typical charging pattern, it gives him a head's up that the employee is likely moving on soon!

Set up

The Chart of Accounts
Create an account called Charges as a subaccount of your Payroll Liabilities. Use the account type "Other Current Liability."

Note: We don't cover Payroll in this book, since every state and business's needs are different.

Payroll Liabilities	Other Current Liability	0.00
Bonus Draw	Other Current Liability	0.00
Charges	Other Current Liability	0.00
Federal Taxes (941/944)	Other Current Liability	0.00
Federal Unemployment (940)	Other Current Liability	0.00
Garnishment	Other Current Liability	0.00
Payroll Draw	Other Current Liability	0.00
State Employment Taxes	Other Current Liability	0.00
State Income Tax	Other Current Liability	0.00
Wages Payable	Other Current Liability	0.00

The Items List
Create a Service item to track each employee's purchases. These are used on the Daily Sales Receipt and for Payroll.

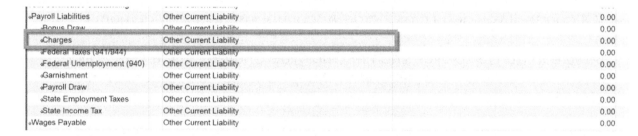

Employee Charges		Service	Sales Income:Sales-Tobacco
Anna's Employe...	Anna's Employee Charges	Service	Payroll Liabilities:Charges
Betty's Employee...	Betty's Employee Charges	Service	Payroll Liabilities:Charges
Cindy's Employe...	Cindy's Employee Charges	Service	Payroll Liabilities:Charges
David's Employe...	David's Employee Charges	Service	Payroll Liabilities:Charges
Frank's Employe...	Frank's Employee Charges	Service	Payroll Liabilities:Charges
George's Employ...	George's Employee Charges	Service	Payroll Liabilities:Charges
Heather's Emplo...	Heather's Employee Charges	Service	Payroll Liabilities:Charges
Ivan's Employee ...	Ivan's Employee Charges	Service	Payroll Liabilities:Charges
Jennifer's Emplo...	Jennifer's Employee Charges	Service	Payroll Liabilities:Charges
Owner's Fuel	Owner's Fuel purchases	Service	Automobile Expense

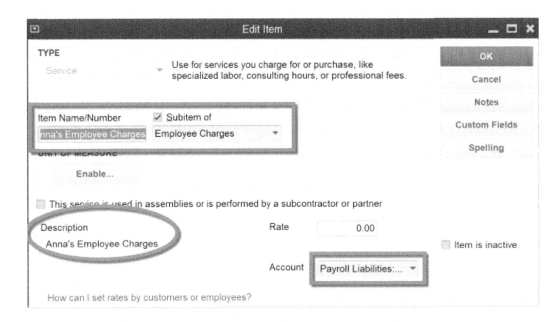

If you are using our ready-made template, ten employee placeholders have been created for you. Change the names to your employees. Delete any extras, or add new ones if needed.

(Of course, if you don't run Charge Accounts, just delete all of them!)

Be sure to put "[Employee's name] Employee Charges" in the Description Memo, because the reports look for this specific name in order to run properly.

For the account, point to the "Payroll Liabilities: Charges" account. This accumulates all of the charges in one place so they appear on the Balance Sheet, and zeros out the total during your payroll runs each month.

Payroll
When you set up your Payroll, point its Employee Charges to the Payroll Liabilities: Charges account.

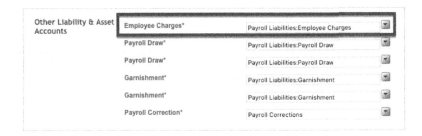

The Monthly Reports

Every month, deduct the employees' accumulated charges from their pay. To know how much to deduct, there are two types of Memorized Reports.

Note that these instructions talk about monthly payroll, but you are welcome to take these steps biweekly or weekly, depending on your payroll frequency.

Last Month's Employee Charges

This report is a summary of all goods charged by Employees the previous month. Use it to confirm that your QuickBooks matches your POS system, and to see how much of your sales are internal.

04/12/2018	Sales Receipt	992	No	Daily Sales	George's Employee Charges	Payroll Liabilities:Employee Charges	Undeposited Funds	-42.56	-36,759.41
04/15/2018	Sales Receipt	999	No	Daily Sales	George's Employee Charges	Payroll Liabilities:Employee Charges	Undeposited Funds	-39.57	-36,798.98
04/17/2018	Sales Receipt	1002	No	Daily Sales	George's Employee Charges	Payroll Liabilities:Employee Charges	Undeposited Funds	-34.00	-36,832.98
04/19/2018	Sales Receipt	1006	No	Daily Sales	George's Employee Charges	Payroll Liabilities:Employee Charges	Undeposited Funds	-20.28	-36,853.26
04/21/2018	Sales Receipt	1011	No	Daily Sales	George's Employee Charges	Payroll Liabilities:Employee Charges	Undeposited Funds	-71.99	-36,925.25
04/23/2018	Sales Receipt	1014	No	Daily Sales	George's Employee Charges	Payroll Liabilities:Employee Charges	Undeposited Funds	-17.29	-36,942.54
04/26/2018	Sales Receipt	1020	No	Daily Sales	George's Employee Charges	Payroll Liabilities:Employee Charges	Undeposited Funds	-17.29	-36,959.83
04/28/2018	Sales Receipt	1025	No	Daily Sales	George's Employee Charges	Payroll Liabilities:Employee Charges	Undeposited Funds	-37.29	-36,997.12
04/30/2018	Sales Receipt	1029	No	Daily Sales	George's Employee Charges	Payroll Liabilities:Employee Charges	Undeposited Funds	-33.21	-37,030.33
04/01/2018	Sales Receipt	968	No	Daily Sales	Heather's Employee Charges	Payroll Liabilities:Employee Charges	Undeposited Funds	-32.02	-37,062.35
04/05/2018	Sales Receipt	978	No	Daily Sales	Heather's Employee Charges	Payroll Liabilities:Employee Charges	Undeposited Funds	-7.16	-37,069.51
04/07/2018	Sales Receipt	983	No	Daily Sales	Heather's Employee Charges	Payroll Liabilities:Employee Charges	Undeposited Funds	-12.40	-37,081.91
04/10/2018	Sales Receipt	988	No	Daily Sales	Heather's Employee Charges	Payroll Liabilities:Employee Charges	Undeposited Funds	-2.99	-37,084.90
04/12/2018	Sales Receipt	992	No	Daily Sales	Heather's Employee Charges	Payroll Liabilities:Employee Charges	Undeposited Funds	-5.57	-37,090.47
04/14/2018	Sales Receipt	997	No	Daily Sales	Heather's Employee Charges	Payroll Liabilities:Employee Charges	Undeposited Funds	-20.00	-37,110.47
04/15/2018	Sales Receipt	999	No	Daily Sales	Heather's Employee Charges	Payroll Liabilities:Employee Charges	Undeposited Funds	-8.56	-37,119.03
04/23/2018	Sales Receipt	1014	No	Daily Sales	Heather's Employee Charges	Payroll Liabilities:Employee Charges	Undeposited Funds	-21.69	-37,140.72
04/25/2018	Sales Receipt	1018	No	Daily Sales	Heather's Employee Charges	Payroll Liabilities:Employee Charges	Undeposited Funds	-7.66	-37,148.38
04/29/2018	Sales Receipt	1027	No	Daily Sales	Heather's Employee Charges	Payroll Liabilities:Employee Charges	Undeposited Funds	-13.15	-37,161.53
04/02/2018	Sales Receipt	970	No	Daily Sales	Josh's Employee Charges	Payroll Liabilities:Employee Charges	Undeposited Funds	-33.35	-37,194.88
04/03/2018	Sales Receipt	972	No	Daily Sales	Josh's Employee Charges	Payroll Liabilities:Employee Charges	Undeposited Funds	-5.08	-37,199.96
04/04/2018	Sales Receipt	976	No	Daily Sales	Josh's Employee Charges	Payroll Liabilities:Employee Charges	Undeposited Funds	-2.04	-37,202.00
04/05/2018	Sales Receipt	978	No	Daily Sales	Josh's Employee Charges	Payroll Liabilities:Employee Charges	Undeposited Funds	-7.61	-37,209.61

To create the Total Employee Charges report the first time:
1. Run a Balance Sheet with the Date range "Last Month."
2. Click on the Customize button.
3. Click on Filter.

4. Click on Account.
5. Choose the Payroll Liabilities: Charges Account.
6. Click OK.
7. Memorize the report. Name it Monthly: Employee Charges.

Individual Employee Charges

You also need separate reports for what each employee purchased from the store, to be used for Payroll Deductions. This report filters by Payroll Liabilities: Charges, and the Employee name in the Memo field.

Be sure to be consistent and avoid typos in the Employee's name, or those entries won't show up on this report!

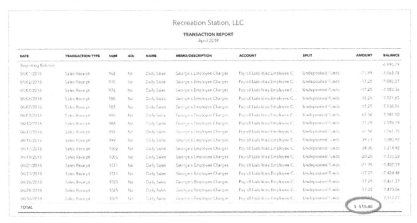

To create this report, follow the same steps from the Monthly Charges on page 46, and also add a Filter for Memo. Enter in the Employee's first name.

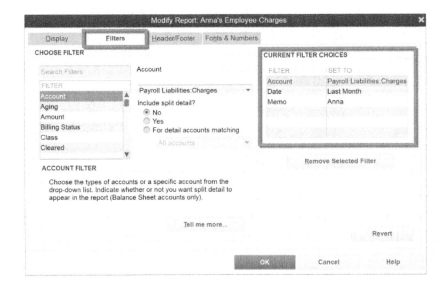

That searches all the transactions for just that one person (again, be sure that the employee's name is spelled the same way in all the Daily Sales Receipts!).

Once this report has been memorized, duplicate it and edit them for all your other Employees.

If you are using our pre-made template, the report has already been created for Employees #1 & 2, Anna and Betty. Duplicate the report and edit the Filter - Memo for additional employees.

Workflow

Daily: Include the employee charges on the Daily Sales Receipt Z-Tape
When you run the Memorized Transaction for your Daily Sales, include the day's total charges incurred for each employee. Their charge account is treated like a Payment Method, and is negative. This puts the money in the Payroll Expense: Charges Other Current Liability account on your Balance Sheet.

Sales Receipt					DATE	SOLD TO	
				MORE	04/17/2018	Daily Sales	
CASH	CHECK	CREDIT DEBIT	e-CHECK		SALE NO. 1		
							CHECK NO.
ITEM	DESCRIPTION				QTY	RATE	AMOUNT
Sales:Grocery Sales	Grocery Sales					0.00	0.00
Sales:Alcohol Sales	Alcohol Sales					0.00	0.00
Sales:ATV Permits	ATV Permits					0.00	0.00
Sales:Deli Sales	Deli Sales					0.00	0.00
Sales:Gas Sales	Gas Sales					0.00	0.00
Sales:Growler Sales	Growler Sales					0.00	0.00
Sales:Lottery Sales	Lottery Sales					0.00	0.00
Sales:Non-Food S...	Non-Food Sales					0.00	0.00
Sales:DFW Sales	DFW Permit Sales					0.00	0.00
Sales:Sporting Go...	Sporting Goods Sales					0.00	0.00
Sales:Tobacco Sal...	Tobacco Sales					0.00	0.00
Credit Card Total	Daily Credit Card Batch, no Wex					-0.01	-0.01
Payment Methods...	Wex Payments					-0.01	-0.01
Payment Methods...	Charge Account for Local business #1					-0.01	-0.01
Payment Methods...	Charge Account for Local Business #2					-0.01	-0.01
Employee Charge...	Owner's Fuel purchases					-0.01	-0.01
Employee Charge...	Owner's Employee Charges					-0.01	-0.01
Employee Charge...	Anna's Employee Charges					-0.01	-0.01
Employee Charge...	Betty's Employee Charges					-0.01	-0.01
Employee Charge...	Cindy's Employee Charges					-0.01	-0.01
Employee Charge...	David's Employee Charges					-0.01	-0.01
Employee Charge...	Frank's Employee Charges					-0.01	-0.01
Employee Charge...	George's Employee Charges					-0.01	-0.01
Employee Charge...	Heather's Employee Charges					-0.01	-0.01
Employee Charge...	Ivan's Employee Charges					-0.01	-0.01
Employee Charge...	Jennifer's Employee Charges					-0.01	-0.01

Reports for Payroll

These reports are marked as monthly, but if you run weekly or biweekly payroll, rename them to your desired frequency, and use them for every payroll run.

Run all the reports above. Use the individual employee reports to fill in their paycheck deductions.

When you run Payroll, the paycheck removes the Liability from the account.

I like to reconcile the Payroll Liabilities: Charges to $0 every month to make sure no charges were missed.

Owner's Charges

How to deduct the owner's fuel fill-ups depends on whether the vehicle is owned by the company or the owner personally. In the case of Recreation Station, the owner's gas was tracked as an Auto Expense for the company vehicle.

If there is no company vehicle, gas charges should be deducted from Payroll, just as they are for other employees. Code them to Owner's Draw if the owner is not on payroll.

Adjusting Errors

If for some reason an employee's charges didn't hit payroll and you need to write them off to Bad Debt, use this Adjusting Journal Entry.

Employee Credit Cards

Add your company credit cards to your Chart of Accounts.

When you have a corporate card with subcards, use the structure below. Add all additional cards, even if they are rarely used.

If you are using our pre-made template, change the name "Chase Visa" to your credit card company. Change "Employee Card #1/2/3" to each of your employee cards, using names and the last four digits of the card numbers to easily tell which card is which (i.e., "David - 7809").

Chase Visa	Credit Card
Employee Card #1	Credit Card
Employee Card #2	Credit Card
Employee Card #3	Credit Card

Only connect the subcards to the Banking Feed. That pulls in each employee's transactions onto their own individual card.

At the end of month, transfer each card's accumulated balance to the MAIN Corp account to zero out the employee's charges. That way your Balance Sheet always shows the actual liability each employee has accumulated[2].

Every month, only reconcile the main account. It gathers all of the subcards' charges together in one place. You will also see the individual cards' balance transfers, both as payment and expense. Check them off, too, since they zero each other out.

---

[2] Visit http://royl.ws/QBO-corporate-credit-cards for a demonstration video.

House Accounts

If local businesses set up Charge Accounts with you and then pay their bills monthly, this is the system for tracking their purchases and invoicing them at the end of the month.

Set up

The Chart of Accounts

Create an Other Current Asset account for each business, using the business's actual name. This shows how much money they owe you.

House Accounts	Other Current Asset	0.02
Local Business #1	Other Current Asset	0.01
Local Business #2	Other Current Asset	0.01

The Items List

These Items are used on the Daily Sales Z-Tape to show how you received payment.

Payment Methods		Service	Sales Income:Sales-Tobacco
ATM Added Funds	ATM Added Funds	Service	Cash on Hand:Cash in ATM
Cash Over and Short	Cash Over/Short (positive for overs, negative...	Service	Cash Over and Short
Charges Local Business #1	Charge Account for Local Business #1	Service	House Accounts:Local Business #1
Charges Local Business #2	Charge Account for Local Business #2	Service	House Accounts:Local Business #2

Create a **Payment Method** for each of the business's Charge Accounts. Include the same business names as above.

Point the Income account to the Other Current Asset account you created above.

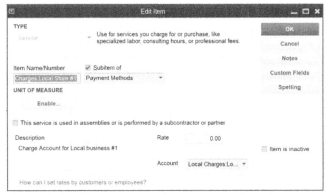

Figure 2: Desktop

Figure 2: QBO

The Monthly Report

Every month, bill each Local Business for their accumulated charges. To know how much to invoice them, run this memorized report.

To create the report the first time:
1. Run a Balance Sheet with the Date range "Last Month."
2. Click on the Customize button.
3. Click on Filter.
4. Click on Account.
5. Choose the Local Business Other Current Asset Account.
6. Click OK.
7. Memorize the report. Name it Monthly: [Name of Business] Monthly Charges.

Once this report has been memorized, duplicate it for all your other House Accounts.

Workflow

Daily: Include their payments on the Daily Sales Receipt Z-Tape

When you run the Memorized Transaction for your Daily Sales, include the day's total charges incurred for each local business. Their credit account is treated like a Payment Method, and will be negative. This puts the money in their Other Current Asset account on your Balance Sheet.

Monthly: Invoice your Local Businesses with Balances

At the end of the month, create an invoice for each local business billing them for that month's charges.

Run the Report
Be sure to invoice them for the new charges for the month, NOT their total activity. The grand total summarizes the *activity* for the month, not how much they owe you. The Memorized Report does not include cumulative charges, only the current month.

If they have one or more open invoices in Accounts Receivable, be sure to send them a Statement in addition to the current invoice.

First, run each Local Charges Memorized Report to see if any of your local companies with Charge Accounts ran up a balance. Run this report on an Accrual basis to see what you haven't yet invoiced. If you run your reports by Cash basis, then your report total balance shows what they haven't paid, whether or not you have invoiced them. This runs the risk of invoicing them for their entire balance, not just the current month.

Let's look at the report below for clarity. In March, the Masonic Lodge ran up $20 in charges. They were invoiced for the $20 in the beginning of April. Because this report is Accrual-based, the invoice zeros out their balance...whether or not they have actually paid! Run an Accounts Receivable Report to see whether they have actually paid.

The $21 is the total balance on all activity for the month, new charges minus the invoiced balance. The charges accrued for April are $41, so that is what should go on the upcoming invoice.

Recreation Station, LLC

TRANSACTION REPORT
April 2018

DATE	TRANSACTION TYPE	NUM	NAME	MEMO/DESCRIPTION	AMOUNT	BALANCE
▾ Local Charges						
▾ Masonic Lodge						
Beginning Balance						20.00
04/04/2018	Invoice	975	Masonic Cemetary	Masonic Lodge Local Charges	-20.00	0.00
04/19/2018	Sales Receipt	1006	Daily Sales	Masonic Lodge Local Charges	41.00	41.00
Total for Masonic Lodge					**$21.00**	
Total for Local Charges					**$21.00**	
TOTAL					**$21.00**	

Send them the Invoice

After you've run the Monthly reports to see what the charges are, invoice them for the accumulated balance as shown on your Balance Sheet report for the month.

Use the "Payment Method: Charges Local Store #1" Item created in the first step, and the amount from the running balance in the above report.

This Invoice zeros out the balance shown in your Balance Sheet report for the Other Current Asset.

Memorize the transaction to easily call it up every month, and just change the date and total.

Employee Timecards

The go-to timecard software for QuickBooks and QuickBooks Online is T-Sheets, from T-Sheets.com. T-Sheets fully integrates from right inside the Intuit software, allowing you to import your employees' time directly into Payroll. Employees can enter their hours right from their cell phone, complete with geolocation to make sure they're onsite.

Aaron at Recreation Station chose to implement T-Sheets' Kiosk feature. He mounted an iPad in the back room to serve as a timeclock. When employees punch (tap!) in, it takes their picture so that they can't cover for a late colleague.

When it's time to run Payroll, Aaron reviews, edits, and approves the hours right inside QuickBooks. Because he's using QuickBooks Payroll, the data autopopulates the payroll run.

As a result of this automated system, it only takes Aaron a few minutes to run Payroll every month.

If you're interested in learning more about T-Sheets, please visit http://royl.ws/tsheets. This link gives you a 10% discount!

Memorized Transactions

This system relies on a full set of Memorized Transactions that run on a daily, weekly, monthly, and annual basis. If you are using QuickBooks Online, look for them in Recurring Transactions.

If you are using our ready-made Template, these transactions have already been created and saved for you. If you are building your file from scratch, save each transaction as we describe it in the instructions. Note that we have grouped the transactions into subheadings by the frequency you use them: Daily, Weekly, Monthly, Yearly, and As Needed.

In this template, they are not set to pop up Reminders, but I encourage you edit the groups to turn on Reminders if it helps you stay up to date.

There is also a set of Backups of key memorized transactions, in case you accidentally overwrite one. Be sure to make new backups and save over these if you alter any of the existing templates.

Daily: Daily Sales Receipt Z-Tape
Run this Z-Tape transaction every day to match your Point-of-Sale System. It always equals $0, because the money you make each day is distributed to a variety of bank accounts, Vendors, and Charge Accounts.

Please see the Daily Sales Receipt explanation in the C-Store chapter on page 16.

Daily: ATM Dispensed
It's important to track how much money left the ATM every day. Run the machine's daily report and replicate it using this Memorized Transaction.

See page 36 in the ATM chapter for a detailed explanation.

Weekly: Lottery
Your state lottery will settle up with you every week. Duplicate their weekly report using this Journal Entry. It makes sure you are properly reimbursed for winning ticket payouts using the Clearing Account.

It classifies all the fee income and associated Cost of Goods Sold.

See the Lottery chapter on page 32 for a detailed explanation.

Monthly: Inventory to COGS Adjustment

At the end of each month, use this Monthly Memorized Transaction to create a Journal Entry that moves the cost of items sold out of Inventory and into COGS. The Journal Entry memos contain the percentages used. You should adjust these amounts to match your preferred margin.

See page 18 in the C-Store chapter for details.

Monthly: WEX Fees

If you don't have WEX, use this Memorized Transaction to represent any situation when you have money in a Clearing Account waiting for reimbursement, but the company takes out fees before they pay you.

The reimbursement itself has already been deducted as a daily Transfer when the money hits your bank.

When you reconcile WEX monthly, they charge two fees, the total WEX %, and the per transaction fee. Use this Monthly Memorized Journal Entry to deduct the transaction fees from the WEX Clearing Account.

Together, the daily reimbursement and the monthly fees zero out the Clearing Account.

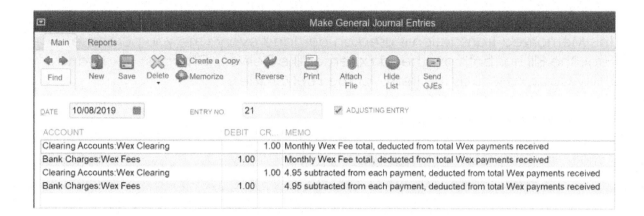

Reconcile WEX Clearing with its Monthly Statement. You can either reconcile it to $0 (challenging because of the delay in payments), or to the offset of what they still haven't paid you as of month's end (but you may have to calculate that by hand).

Monthly: House Charge Account Invoices

If you run House Charge Accounts for local businesses, run these reports to know how much to invoice each company.

See House Accounts on page 54 for instructions.

Yearly (or more often): Inventory Adjustment for Shrinkage

Because your Monthly Inventory Adjustment is based on margin estimates instead of actual inventory counts, it's important to periodically square up your numbers. Use this Adjusting Journal Entry to compensate for theft, loss, or expired products.

I have it titled "Annual," but I recommend you do this quarterly, or as often as you want your reports to be completely accurate!

See page 19 for instructions.

As Needed: Fuel Purchases

This Memorized Transaction is used on-demand every time you purchase Fuel. The Bill has both overhead Expenses like Delivery Charges, Taxes, and Utility Costs, as well as the Items for the Fuel Grades.

Turn to page 22 for instructions.

As Needed: Owner Comped Gift Certificate

When the Owner gives away goods, use this Journal Entry to account for the retail amount. It counts as a discount given, and makes the funds available as a gift certificate to be used as payment.

As Needed: Adjustments to Employee Charges

If you wind up with a discrepancy between accumulated Employee Charges and what you paid out through Payroll, use this Journal Entry to zero it out. ·

See Employee Charge Adjustments on page 50.

Backups

These are simply duplicate copies of key memorized transactions. When you use a Memorized Transaction and change it, QuickBooks may ask if you want to save the changes. If you want those changes to be permanent and appear next time, say yes. But if you don't really want to overwrite your saved transaction, and you accidentally say yes and change it, duplicate this Backup to replace the original.

However, this does mean that you need to keep the Backups current. If you modify one of the Memorized Transactions, don't forget to update the Backup!

Custom Reports

Throughout this book, we've given instructions on Memorized Reports to save.

You may want to also create the additional custom reports below to analyze your business. Edit the report names, filters, and headers to suit your circumstances.

DFW P&L

Create a Year-to-Date report for how much money you made on Department of Fish and Wildlife permits. It's a standard Profit & Loss Statement, filtered for DFW Income and COGS.

Lottery P&L

This Year-to-date report shows how much money you made on the State Lottery. Create a standard Profit & Loss Statement, and filter it for Lottery Income and all the associated COGS and Expense categories.

Employee Charges

These are discussed on page 46. There are two types of Employee Charge Reports:

- *Last Month's Employee Charges* to confirm that your employee charges in QuickBooks match your POS system. It also shows how much of your sales were internal.
- *Individual Monthly Reports* for each employee, to know how much to deduct from the employee's payroll

House Accounts

These are discussed on page 54. Run this report every month to know how much that company charged every month. Be sure to invoice the business for the full amount of purchases for the month, and not the net for the month or their full balance.

Appendices

Appendix 1: Glossary

These terms are used in the Chart of Accounts, Items List, and Memorized Transactions. Edit the names to suit your needs. Delete categories you won't use (after you're sure you don't need them!). Duplicate elements you need more of.

Air Machine
Use to track income from Air & Water machines.

ATM
Includes Bank Account, Fee Income, and Items.
Reconcile ATM Clearing to $0 to confirm money with ATM company.

Bottle Return
If your state has bottle recycling, use these to track returns.

Clearing Account
A Clearing Account is a bank account that doesn't hold money. It's a holding tank, where money goes in, and an equal amount of money goes out.

An example is the ATM. You put money in, and that same money is dispensed.

Periodically reconcile your Clearing Accounts to $0.

COGS
Cost of Goods Sold. In this template, all Item purchases go to Inventory Asset, and you need to use the Monthly Journal Entry to move the cost of items sold into COGS.

Because this template is designed to work with a Point-of-Sale System, use a percentage or spreadsheet to calculate the $ to transfer each month.

The Memorized Transaction memos contain the cost percentages you specify. You should adjust these amounts to your margin. You can, of course, do an actual physical inventory count to move real numbers if you prefer.

The Fuel % should be adjusted based on the average cost of fuel purchased based on the Vendor's reports, Total # Gal purchased * Avg cost delivered per gal.

At the end of the year, there is an Annual Memorized Transaction to correct these estimates based on your actual physical inventory.

Customer Center
Contains placeholder names for common income sources.

All daily income goes to Daily Sales via the Daily Sales Receipt in Memorized Transactions.

Edit or delete these if not needed.

Daily Sales Receipt
Run this Z-Tape every day to replicate your Point-of-Sale System totals. It always equals $0, because the money you make each day is distributed to a variety of bank accounts, Vendors, and Charge Accounts.

DFW
Department of Fish and Wildlife. Use if you sell fishing and access permits.

Employee Charges
When employees charge store purchases and gas to their account, these charges are deducted from Payroll. Change the names to your employees.

There is a Memorized Transaction to use if for some reason the charges didn't hit payroll and you need to write them off.

EVS - Electric Vehicle Station
Use to track income from Electric Vehicle Stations.

Growlers
This store has a department to fill beer growlers. Edit the name if you sell any specialty items, or delete.

House Accounts
If local businesses run a charge account with you, use Local Business #1, Local Business #2, etc. to track their purchases and monthly statements (edit the names to the actual company names).

At the end of the month, run the Memorized Report to see what their balances are.

Then use the Memorized invoice to invoice them for that month's balance.

Incentives

Grocery suppliers and Tobacco companies pay by giving you sales incentives. Includes Income accounts and Items.

Journal Entries

Transactions in QuickBooks used to move money back and forth between Assets, Liabilities, Clearing Accounts, and Expenses.

Lottery

Track Lottery tickets held, sold, and payout redemptions.

Memorized Transaction List

This template relies on a full set of Memorized Transactions that run on a daily, weekly, monthly, and annual basis. In this template, they are not set to pop up Reminders, but I encourage you Edit the Groups to turn on Reminders if it helps you stay up to date.

In QuickBooks Online, Memorized Transactions are called Recurring Transactions.

There is also a set of Backups of key memorized transactions, in case you accidentally overwrite one. Be sure to replace these if you alter any of the main templates.

WEX

Corporate payment system for Gas charges. Includes Clearing Account and Items.

Use Monthly Memorized transaction to deduct both the total WEX % fees, and the per transaction fees.

Reconcile WEX Clearing with WEX's Monthly Statement.

Appendix 2:
Daily Sales Report from a POS System

```
Operator Shift Report
Business Date: 10/5/2019
Report Time:: 10/6/2019 7:38:29 PM
Cashier: Flores, Amanda

    Shift Id:  1
       Start:  10/5/2019 5:04:20 AM
         End:  10/5/2019 12:33:33 PM
Last Term ID:  1

     System Gross (+Tax)        1165.95
------------------------------------------------
Discounts and Refunds:
   0 Discounts            0.00(-)
   0 Refund Discount      0.00(+)
     Net Discounts                   0.00(-)
   0 Coupons              0.00(-)
   0 Refund Coupons       0.00(+)
     Net Coupons                     0.00(-)
  26 AutoDetect Disc     21.83(-)
   0 Refund AutoDete      0.00(+)
     Net AutoDetect Disc.           21.83(-)
   0 Sales Refunds (+tax)            0.00(-)
------------------------------------------------
     Net Sales (+tax)            1144.12
     Sales Tax                      0.00(-)
     Net Sales (-tax)            1144.12(=)
  97 Sales Count
     Avg Gross Transaction         12.02
------------------------------------------------
Non Cash Tender Totals:
  16 Credit               214.33
  16 Debit                224.94
   1 EBT                    3.70
   1 1Shane Piper          15.00
     Non Cash Totals       457.97
================================================
     Net Sales (+tax)            1144.12
   1 Start Amount               170.64(+)
   0 Paid Ins                     0.00(+)
   0 Local Acct Payments          0.00(+)
   0 Drawer Loans                 0.00(+)
   1 Drawer Pickups               0.00(-)
   1 Paid Outs                    0.50(-)
   1 End Amount                 170.64(-)
     Total Tenders Due          1143.62(=)
------------------------------------------------
Tender Over/(Short):
Credit
  16 Credit            (214.33)
  16 Credit Total                (214.33)
Debit
  16 Debit             (224.94)
  16 Debit Total                 (224.94)
EBT Recon
   1 EBT                 (3.70)
   1 EBT Recon Total               (3.70)
Shane Piper
   1 1Shane Piper       (15.00)
   1 Shane Piper Total            (15.00)
Cash
     Cash Total                  (685.65)
================================================
   0 No Sale Transactions
  18 Item Deletions               69.65
```

Item Level Sales Report

Detail: Data Not Finalized (Site)
Department Sales

Site: Recreation Station (0001)   **Start date:** 10/5/2019   **End date:** 10/5/2019

Department	Sold Qty	Sold Amt	Item Reductions ($)	Refunds ($)	Net Sales	Percent of Net Sales
Alcohol	107.00	531.18	3.32	0.00	527.86	4.28%
Automotive	4.00	19.86	0.00	0.00	19.86	0.16%
Beverages	363.00	727.37	65.91	0.00	661.46	5.36%
Candy	57.00	87.75	0.28	0.00	87.47	0.71%
Coffee	24.00	33.06	0.00	0.00	33.06	0.27%
Deli	198.00	610.84	9.00	0.00	601.84	4.88%
Fuel	2,484.41	8,273.24	0.00	0.00	8,273.24	67.10%
Grocery	15.00	46.98	0.00	0.00	46.98	0.38%
Growler	6.00	48.97	0.00	0.00	48.97	0.40%
Health	3.00	8.47	0.00	0.00	8.47	0.07%
Lottery	32.00	162.00	0.00	0.00	162.00	1.31%
Non-Food	31.00	53.61	0.00	0.00	53.61	0.43%
QDFW Permit	7.00	227.50	0.00	0.00	227.50	1.85%
Snacks	119.00	254.87	0.00	0.00	254.87	2.07%
Sporting Goods	8.00	118.49	0.00	0.00	118.49	0.96%
Tobacco	165.00	1,204.95	0.60	0.00	1,204.35	9.77%
Total:	**3,623.41**	**12,409.14**	**79.11**	**0.00**	**12,330.03**	**100.00%**

POS Z-Tape

Cashier Report

Site: Recreation Station (0001)

Metric	Value
Gross Sales ($)	12,409.14
Refund ($)	0.00
Refund Count (#)	0
Coupon ($)	0.00
Coupon Count (#)	0
Discount ($)	(9.00)
Discount Count (#)	3
Special ($)	(70.11)
Special Count (#)	80
Net Sales ($)	12,330.03
Non-Sales Debit ($)	0.00
Non-Sales Debit Count (#)	0
Non-Sales Credit ($)	0.00
Non-Sales Credit Count (#)	0
Pay In ($)	0.00
Pay Out ($)	74.70
Daily Over/Short ($)	(3,646.89)
Avg Gross Sale ($)	18.66
Customer Count (#)	665
VAT ($)	0.00
Tax ($)	0.00
No Sale Count (#)	0
CSS Void Item ($)	0.00
CSS Void Item Count (#)	0
POS Void Item ($)	99.30
POS Void Item Count (#)	30

Cashier Report

Site: Recreation Station (0001)

Metric	Value
Void Transaction ($)	3.69
Void Transaction Count (#)	15
Non-Cash Tender Total ($)	8,029.38
Non-Cash Tender Count (#)	312
Credit Total ($)	6,835.97
Credit Count Total (#)	219
Debit Total ($)	982.94
Debit Count Total (#)	68
EBT - Food Stamp Total ($)	81.98
EBT - Food Stamp Count Total (#)	11
Manufacturer Account Total ($)	1.50
Manufacuterer Account Count Total (#)	3
Others Total ($)	126.99
Others Count Total (#)	11
Money Order ($)	0.00
Money Order Count (#)	0
Collected Fee ($)	0.00
Collected Fee Count (#)	0
Lottery ($)	0.00
Lottery (#)	0
Winners - Free Tickets ($)	0.00
Winners - Cash Winner ($)	0.00
Fuel Sales ($)	8,273.24
Fuel Volume	2,484.407
Fuel Sales Count (#)	236
Drive Off ($)	(

Appendix 3:
A Detailed Convenience Store Category List

The C-Store/Gas Station in Florida that we worked with wanted a more detailed list of products sold in order to track profitability.

Here are their sample categories in the Chart of Accounts. The colons indicate subcategories.

Most companies mirror the structure in your Sales Income, Inventory Assets, Cost of Goods Sold, and Items list. It's also possible to have this much detail on your Inventory Asset and Items lists, but point them to the root categories in the Sales Income and/or COGS.

Inventory	Other Current Assets	Inventory
Inventory:Inventory - Store	Other Current Assets	Inventory
Inventory:Inventory - Store:Inventory-Alcohol	Other Current Assets	Other Current Assets
Inventory:Inventory - Store:Inventory-Alcohol:Inventory-Beer	Other Current Assets	Other Current Assets
Inventory:Inventory - Store:Inventory-Alcohol:Inventory-Wine	Other Current Assets	Other Current Assets
Inventory:Inventory - Store:Inventory-CStore	Other Current Assets	Other Current Assets
Inventory:Inventory - Store:Inventory-CStore:Inventory-Automotive	Other Current Assets	Other Current Assets
Inventory:Inventory - Store:Inventory-CStore:Inventory-Candy Gum	Other Current Assets	Other Current Assets
Inventory:Inventory - Store:Inventory-CStore:Inventory-Deli	Other Current Assets	Other Current Assets
Inventory:Inventory - Store:Inventory-CStore:Inventory-Drinks	Other Current Assets	Other Current Assets
Inventory:Inventory - Store:Inventory-CStore:Inventory-Drinks:Inventory-Energy Drinks	Other Current Assets	Other Current Assets
Inventory:Inventory - Store:Inventory-CStore:Inventory-Drinks:Inventory-Fountain	Other Current Assets	Other Current Assets
Inventory:Inventory - Store:Inventory-CStore:Inventory-Drinks:Inventory-Juice	Other Current Assets	Other Current Assets
Inventory:Inventory - Store:Inventory-CStore:Inventory-Drinks:Inventory-Soft Drinks	Other Current Assets	Other Current Assets
Inventory:Inventory - Store:Inventory-CStore:Inventory-Drinks:Inventory-Teas	Other Current Assets	Other Current Assets
Inventory:Inventory - Store:Inventory-CStore:Inventory-Drinks:Inventory-Water	Other Current Assets	Other Current Assets
Inventory:Inventory - Store:Inventory-CStore:Inventory-Fruit	Other Current Assets	Other Current Assets
Inventory:Inventory - Store:Inventory-CStore:Inventory-Gift Cards	Other Current Assets	Other Current Assets
Inventory:Inventory - Store:Inventory-CStore:Inventory-Grocery	Other Current Assets	Other Current Assets
Inventory:Inventory - Store:Inventory-CStore:Inventory-Ice and Ice Cream	Other Current Assets	Other Current Assets
Inventory:Inventory - Store:Inventory-CStore:Inventory-Snacks Alternative	Other Current Assets	Other Current Assets
Inventory:Inventory - Store:Inventory-CStore:Inventory-Snacks Salty	Other Current Assets	Other Current Assets
Inventory:Inventory - Store:Inventory-CStore:Inventory-Snacks Sweet	Other Current Assets	Other Current Assets
Inventory:Inventory - Store:Inventory-CStore:Inventory-Store Supplies	Other Current Assets	Other Current Assets
Inventory:Inventory - Store:Inventory-Lottery	Other Current Assets	Other Current Assets
Inventory:Inventory - Store:Inventory-Lottery:Inventory-Lotto	Other Current Assets	Other Current Assets
Inventory:Inventory - Store:Inventory-Lottery:Inventory-Scratch offs	Other Current Assets	Other Current Assets
Inventory:Inventory - Store:Inventory-Tobacco	Other Current Assets	Other Current Assets
Inventory:Inventory - Store:Inventory-Tobacco:Inventory-Cigarettes	Other Current Assets	Other Current Assets
Inventory:Inventory - Store:Inventory-Tobacco:Inventory-Tobacco Other	Other Current Assets	Other Current Assets
Inventory:Inventory-Fuel	Other Current Assets	Other Current Assets
Inventory:Inventory-Fuel:Inventory-Fuel-Diesel	Other Current Assets	Inventory
Inventory:Inventory-Fuel:Inventory-Fuel-Regular	Other Current Assets	Inventory
Inventory:Inventory-Fuel:Inventory-Fuel-Super	Other Current Assets	Inventory

Appendix 4:
Do you need more
QuickBooks training?

Take our QuickBooks Online Video Course at www.royalwise.com

This book provides a template for setting up QuickBooks, but it assumes that you have bookkeeping and/or QuickBooks experience.

If you need additional instruction on how to use QuickBooks or QuickBooks Online, we provide in-depth training. Would you like to see the information come to life?

- Watch a 3-hour video course covering the material in this book at **http://royl.ws/Gas-Cstore**.

- Learn to use QuickBooks Online or QuickBooks Desktop with our On-Demand Courses containing how-to videos, broken up into short clips. Take a look at **http://royl.ws/QuickBooks-training-videos**.

Our website is the perfect reference library when a specific question pops up during your workday and you need a fast answer!

Watch today!

About Royalwise Solutions

Royalwise Solutions, Inc. at www.royalwise.com is a husband-and-wife computer support company focused on teaching you business solutions to enhance your productivity.

Alicia and Jamie Pollock are certified in:
- QuickBooks
- Microsoft Office (Word, Excel, Outlook, PowerPoint, Access)
- Apple Macintosh, iPhones, iPads

We visit your home or office, or do screen shares anywhere in the world. We get you set up with your new software, troubleshoot what's not working, and answer all your questions.

Book an appointment at **http://royl.ws/schedule-with-Alicia.**

Call us at 503-406-6550!

Training Classes are available to fit your needs:
- 1-on-1
- Small groups
- Corporate Trainings
- Public Classes and Webinars

Find us on these social media websites as well:

YouTube: Getthemaxfromyourmac

Facebook: RoyalwiseSolutions

Twitter: @royalwise

Index

Notes

Made in the USA
Monee, IL
08 November 2020